HOW TO BECOME A DAY TRADER

Strategies on how to get what you want.

A day trade start guide for a successful day trader

Learn how day trade for a living is possible and made it easy.

Table of Contents

Conclusion

Introduction

If you can't get a seat at a prop firm, you can still be a day trader - and this is much more likely to be your situation when you're starting out in day trading. Most day traders work from home, on their own time, with their own resources. In general, people who trade from home are referred to as "retail" traders. Since this is probably going to be your situation as a novice day trader, let's go over all the things you need to get started with day trading:

Capital: it's a cliché: "you need to have money to make money." But, it's true. To start day trading, you will need to have some money to get started - whether that's a few hundred dollars or a few thousand. How much capital you need depends on how you plan to trade, and what type of assets you plan to trade in. Most brokerage firms will have a minimum balance requirement before you get started.

Under the rule, you are generally required to have at least $5,000 to invest in order to day trade stocks. However, there are various strategies you can follow to avoid the rule, and we'll discuss those in detail later. It's also important to note that the rule only applies to stocks, so if you are day trading futures, options, or currencies, you do not have to meet that capital limit.

One more thing on capital: you should only invest with money that you can afford to lose. While it's possible to make huge profits as a day trader, trading is inherently risky, and you have to be prepared to lose everything you put in. However, by carefully planning and following the guidance in this book, you can minimize the chance of disaster and find the path to profitability.

A Day Trading Brokerage: in order to trade stocks or most other assets, you'll need to create an account with a brokerage firm. Your broker is your connection to the market. While many large banks operate investment accounts that you could use for day trading, you probably want to get set up with a brokerage that targets day traders using an account that's designed for day trading.

Some of the most popular online brokerages for day trading are: Interactive Brokers, TradeStation Lightspeed Trading, TD Ameritrade, Fidelity, eTrade, OptionsXpress, SpeedTrader, Generic Trade and MB Trading. Each company has its own advantages and disadvantages, offering access to different markets and asset classes, requiring different amounts of starting capital, and each has its own fee structure to deal with.

While picking a brokerage is very important, it shouldn't be the first decision you make as a new trader. First you should decide on a trading plan, familiarize yourself with stock charts and the tools described in this chapter, and only then should you look at brokerage accounts to see which firm best matches your needs and your trading plan. When in doubt, however, it's hard to go wrong with a well-known name like eTrade or TD Ameritrade.

Chapter 1
Life of Day Trader

A lot of retail traders operate from a small home office. Others work in regular offices but remain small traders with limited funds but sufficient trading equipment. As a day trader, there is basically no boss or supervisor to tell a trader what to do. Nobody watches over them or bosses them around. This means a trader has the freedom to organize and manage their trading days.

Because of this freedom, day traders need to exercise a lot of discipline. Traders need to wake up early and prepare for the trading day. Mental preparation is part of a trader's morning ritual before, during, or after breakfast. It is advisable to be up a couple of hours before the trading day begins and ensure everything is in place. There are a couple of things that generally need to be achieved.

1. As soon as breakfast is made, the trader should rehearse their strategies in their minds and probably on paper too. Sometimes it is necessary to run a strategy on a demo platform. Also, a good plan should be made and followed to the letter. This plan includes how much money to place on a trade, which points to exit a trade, when to take profits, and so on.

2. Traders need to check and confirm their trading accounts and the amounts therein. It is crucial that a trader knows the amount available for trading purposes so they know the amounts they can spend per trade. It is recommended that traders should not spend more than 2% of their trading capital on a single trade. The accepted range is between 1% and 2% of the account balance. Beginners with no prior trading experience

should not spend more than 1% of their trading balance per trade. Also, a trader should exit their positions three minutes prior to a major financial or economic announcement.

3.It is advisable to always or regularly check the financial calendar and note any major events. Any such events should be clearly marked onto the calendar and reminds initiated. These events have major implications for stocks and activity at the markets.

It is crucial that day traders learn how to select the best stocks to trade. This is because the stocks chosen for day trading will pretty much determine the outcome of your trading ventures. As such, choosing the correct stocks ensures that you fare better at the markets and maximize on profitability.

Identifying Stocks for Day Trading

1. Funds Available

The first instance is to take cognizance of a trader's financial position. Depending on the number of funds available, you can determine the stocks to choose. There is a wide variety of stocks to choose from. However, you can only choose as much as your funds allow you.

You also need to consider the amount of risk you can tolerate. Generally, the amount of risk a trader is willing to take the more they stand to win. Traders also need to consider buying a security in a field or industry that they are familiar with. For instance, an accountant may be happy trading financial stocks while an engineer will be at home with tech stocks, and so on. Such considerations will ensure you understand what is going on in the industry, and this will boost trading ventures.

Liquidity

Traders also need to find securities that are highly liquid and trade in large volumes. There is a reason for this. When a security is trading in high volumes, then it is easy to enter and exit positions. Also, highly liquid securities make it easy to get paid upon exiting a position. Some of the best financial securities that have large volumes and are liquid are blue-chip stocks. These are stocks of highly valued companies that are constantly making large profits, are stable, and considered very valuable.

Stocks that are highly liquid tend to be more easily traded and are easier to discount compared to many others. Also, stocks and securities from firms with large volumes of shares traded tend to be more favorable. Traders should take the time to conduct analysis in order to find which stocks are most suitable. A good stock is one from a large-cap company rather than a low cap firm. This is because it is easier to find buyers of large volume stocks compared with buyers for low volume stocks.

Volatility

Some of the best instruments are highly volatile ones. Volatile stocks and securities provide day traders a chance to capitalize on the rapid and numerous price changes. Remember that day; traders make most of their money due to the rapid or frequent price changes. As such, stocks that are constantly moving up and down or are volatile are much better and preferable compared to less volatile ones.

We have what is known as the TVI or trade volume index. This is a measure of the volumes of a particular stock that is trading at the market. Using this index, traders can determine whether or not to choose the particular stock. TVI indicates the total amount of cash that is following into and out o stock. The volume gives a clear indication of the stock's activity at the markets.

Industry

Another crucial aspect to consider when selecting a stock is the industry. One of the best industries for day traders should be the financial services sector. This sector is excellent because it features most of the above factors like large volumes and volatility. A great example, in this case, is Microsoft Corp. This is a well-established company with a large global market, growing income, and a positive reputation.

Microsoft Corp also happens to be among the most highly traded stocks. This is why it is among the most preferred stock by most day traders. It is definitely an excellent choice for day trading forays as it exhibits all the desired characteristics. Bank of America is a large corporation, it trades a large volume of shares each day, its stock is volatile, yet the bank remains stable and profitable through the years.

Emotions

One important point worth mentioning is that a day trader should never let emotions take charge of trading activities. When a trading strategy is formulated, it should be implemented to the letter. All too often, traders either become greedy or despair and then begin trading guided by their emotions.

For instance, they refuse to exit a winning trade instead of collecting profits first. In other cases, traders choose to continue incurring losses beyond the stop-loss point. These are dangerous attributes and are common among new and novice traders. It is a practice that should be shunned at all costs for successful and profitable day trading.

Summary

Day traders execute various intraday strategies in order to benefit from the volatility at the markets. To be effective, the first step should be the identification of suitable stocks to trade.

There are different stocks available in the market. A good trader will conduct an analysis using tools and charts to find the most appropriate stocks. These are stocks with high volumes from stable companies that showcase a fair amount of volatility.

It does not have to stock only. Day traders can also deal with other commodities such as bonds, currencies, futures, and options. Once the trading instrument has been determined, the only other step is to develop a strategy and begin implementing it. A major challenge that numerous traders experience, especially novice and beginners, is that they let their emotions interfere with their trading.

This means that traders take their time to conduct research and come up with a trading strategy only to discard it at the last moment.

Emotional stability is crucial because it is the only way for a trader to successfully execute a strategy and make profits along the way. When emotions take charge, a trader will keep holding on to a falling position beyond the stop-loss point. They will lose money using this approach. However, when winning, they do not take profits as was intended, but instead, they tend to keep at trade and risk losing all their winnings.

Life of a Typical Day Trader

It is commonly believed that the life of a trader is fun and exciting and that they deal in numbers and money all day long. This is far from the truth. A trader's life is not all fun and glam, and they do not really live on the edge. While it is true that they spend the entire trading day dealing in options, stocks, currencies, and other securities, they really do work very hard and tend to focus too much on the markets.

The life of a day trader can actually be exciting simply because of all the numerous events and unexpected occurrences that can take place. But in general, most trading days are quiet with little or no excitement but general trading as usual. There is hardly any action except for reading charts, entering positions, checking news feeds, and so on. Therefore, any glamor that people think exists in day trading is only a figment of the imagination.

You will also find that most day traders, especially small retail traders, trading from their home offices. Many have established a workstation at their home offices from where they do all the work. We also have institutional traders working from fully furnished offices with access to plenty of resources. At any one time, this day, traders will be entering positions in the market and make trades worth hundreds of millions of dollars.

Traders and their Trading Styles

There are different definitions that define traders. For instance, experts sometimes divide traders by the time in which they enter and exit trades. This time is also known as the holding time. At other times, traders can be classified based on the ways in which they identify opportunities and the approach they use to trade these opportunities.

For instance, we have discretionary traders. These are

traders who base their trades on decisions based on certain factors. We also have system traders who are named thus because they automate their trades and use the system to execute their strategies. Other kinds of traders are the day trader, swing trader, scalpers, and high-frequency traders. Based on these definitions, it is clear to observe that there is no typical day trader but a variety of different strategies adopted by different day traders.

How to Take Profits

The whole purpose of trading is to generate profits. So every time a trader trades and the trades earn a profit, these profits need to be consolidated, locked in, and then taken out. If this does not happen, then the profits could disappear and sometimes even turn into a loss.

A good day trader should close all their open trades just before the markets close for the day. One of the best ways of collecting any profits generated is to exit at the close of one trade. There are other ways of taking profits. Learning to do so is essential if you want to be profitable.

1. Take Profits when Price is Close to Strong Resistance or Support

It is advisable to move in and take profits at one of the established points where the price is likely to reverse. If you have a chart, then you can search for points where the stock makes attempts to drop after an upward trend. For instance, fins a suitable support area.

If the trade entered is a short position, then it is advisable to exit just above this support area. Now if the price continues falling, this is not desirable but is something that could happen. A fall in price will break the support, and the trader will have to enter another short trade.

A trend analysis is essential to arrive at the best position to take in profits. If there is a strong upward trend, then resistance is very likely to be overcome compared to other situations such as the range. The trick here is to simply wait and see if the price can overcome the resistance. If it does, then a trader should exit any long positions immediately.

However, should there be a significant downward trend, then the support is highly likely to stay put and not get broken. The trick, in this case, will be to wait and see if the support will sustain the momentum so that more profits can be extracted. Any short trade should be exited should the stock price continue going higher beyond the support area.

The Price can Stall and Reverse

It is possible in some cases for the price to stall and sometimes even make a reversal. It is advisable to study tendencies in order to determine the best exit points. Sometimes it may be profitable to avoid exiting at the resistance and support points. However, in all cases, it is important to always have a determined exit point. If a price continues to increase, then keep watching until it stalls then exit at this point.

In stocks trading a consolidation is also known as a stall. It refers to a collection of three or four price bars which do not progress any trend that existed. When the price momentum stalls, it will indicate on the charts. A trader should locate their exit point just beneath the upper side of the stalled bars. If this is not possible, then an alternative is to exit a trade as soon as the price falls below any one of the three bars.

Basically, consolidation or stall does not necessarily

imply that there will be a price reversal. This may not necessarily be the case. However, it presents an excellentopportunity to take profits.

If a trader is convinced that the upward trend will proceed for a while, then it is advisable to hold on and the only exit once the share price starts to trend downwards and moves below the consolidation point. This is an excellent approach to protecting profits, and it can get better by searching for other exit points further up.

Take out Profits before Major Financial Announcements

All traders are aware of the impact of major economic and financial news on the markets. Depending on the news, stock prices are likely to dip or rise. Such news causes the stock market to be very volatile. Any day trader knows that they should take profits right before any major announcements in the business and finance worlds.

The reason for this is to consolidate any gains and exit the markets profitably. Day traders often focus on capturing the market in its normal conditions throughout any trading day. However, all this could change with a major announcement.

Announcements such as economic release news, payrolls, company losses, and so on can result in huge price moves due to volatility. Taking profits before any such major announcements are generally the norm.

Traders will avoid unnecessary turmoil or risks associated with major announcements. Once a trader exits the markets after the major announcement, the next step would be to review the market and then see how they can capitalize on the resulting movement.

Taking Profits

Traders need to be very attentive to the markets and to actions that may affect the market. Profits are often taken at resistance or support points, and attention is also necessary for such instances. Exiting generally occurs when the momentum slows down or when the trend reverses. There is always the possibility of entering into other trades, but the profit opportunities may not be similar.

Regular and close monitoring of economic news is a must. A good day trader should keep one eye on the news and another on the trading platform. Monitoring economic and business news then exiting a position before the news is released is absolutely essential.

Such events, when announced, can have a huge impact on the markets and taking profits early enough is definitely the best approach. Once the news is released, the trader is free to get back into the market and see what opportunities are present. Also, it is important to know that the scenarios mentioned above do not happen all the time.

Not all day trading sessions will see a relevant support and resistance position or a consolidation point. Therefore, it is advisable to be on the lookout, be disciplined, and learn the best time to take profits and generally have a suitable profit taking plan.

Chapter 2

How Much Do You Need to Day Trade?

Before you begin any business, one would want to know how much they need as capital. The same case applies to day trading. An important question that most investors would want to know is the amount of capital that is required from them. The amount of money that you need to day trade will depend on the market that you wish to invest in. Your style of trading will also have an impact on the amount of money that you need to raise.

Different markets will require varying amounts of capital. Below is an analysis of the different markets that are at your disposal and the respective capital requirements.

Capital Requirements for Stock Traders

If you are going to trade in stocks, then you need to have at least $25,000 saved up for the trading activity. You are not limited to this amount of money. If you wish to trade more than three times, you should consider having more than $30,000. When your trading account falls below $25,000, it would not be possible for you to trade. You will have to top up your account to the minimum balance required. The account balance minimum here only stipulates to traders who would wish to invest in US stocks.

You should realize that the minimum account balance required to invest in other stocks in global markets will vary. The country that you rise in might not have any minimum balance required. Regardless, it is advisable to deposit a reasonable amount that will see you earning good profits for every buying and selling activity that you engage in. Why are we saying this? There are instances where lower balances will only be eaten up by commissions and transaction costs. Therefore, you will not notice any changes in your account because of these deductions.

Lack of capital will always be a problem for most traders in the market. Insufficient capital will prevent you from taking advantage of market volatility. You might have incurred losses now, but later you could recover your money when the stocks unexpectedly rise. As such, having sufficient capital comes highly recommended.

Capital Requirements for Forex Traders

The forex market is somewhat different from the stock market. In this case, smaller amounts of capital are required. So, for a newbie like you, this should be good news. With the little capital that you have saved up, you can begin day trading in forex today. The advantage of forex is that you can exploit the leverage provided of up to 50:1. This could even go higher in certain nations. An increase in leverage implies that there is a higher risk that could be met with a remarkable reward.

Forex trading stands as an ideal choice for day trading due to its liquidity. The forex market is the largest market globally. Usually, the money in circulation on a daily basis goes up to $5 trillion. Therefore, the liquidity aspect of this market makes it quite appealing. So, how much money do you need to begin forex trading? With as little as $100, you can kick off trading. Nevertheless, a recommended figure is $500.

This gives you the opportunity of buying currencies with ideal stop levels.

As you can see, this is a small amount of money which you will require to begin this activity. You cannot claim that you will make a living out of it. It is, however, important to remember that you can gradually raise capital with the daily incomes that you earn. In line with this, you should never overlook the importance of starting small simply because you are new to forex trading.

Capital Requirements for Futures

Besides investing in stocks and forex, you will also have the option of investing in futures. The good thing about futures is that you can invest in it with minimal capital requirements. There is no legal minimum balance that you should have so as to invest in futures. However, it is important for a trader to have enough capital to cover day trading margins within a particular day. A good number of brokers will require a trader to have a minimum balance of $1,000. If you are trading E-mini S&P 500 (ES) futures, brokers will demand a minimum balance of $400. This is the day trading margin that you will be limited to. Regardless of the fact that you are not limited to a specific balance, you should strive to begin with a realistic balance of at least $8,000. There are other futures that your broker will want additional margins for you to trade effectively. Hence, you ought to confirm with your trader before signing up for anything.

On a final word concerning the amount of money that you need, it is clear that different markets will require varying capital amounts. If you are running on a tight budget, trading in stocks is not advisable as it is capital intensive. On the other hand, forex gives you the flexibility of starting trading with as little as $1,000. Nonetheless, it is recommended for you to have more to warrant that you have a buffer. Futures is also a great option when working with limited funds.

It should also be made clear that it is never wise to trade with your capital at first. When working with a broker, make good use of demo accounts to trade with virtual money. Once you notice that your trading strategies suit you, you can move forward to use real money. The advantage gained here is that you can easily identify possible mistakes that you could make when using your money. As such, it saves you from risking with your hard-earned cash.

Defining Your Risk Tolerance

Aside from knowing the amount of money you will need to trade, you also should pause for a while and define your risk tolerance. What do we mean by risk tolerance? It refers to the degree of unpredictability in investment returns which a trader is willing to endure. As a trader, you ought to have an in-depth understanding of how much you can withstand the large market swings. There are times where you might panic when markets seem to be falling. In such cases, you might end up selling at the wrong time. Therefore, this is where you should be aware of your risk tolerance. How much can you stomach in day trading?

To clearly define your tolerance capacity, you should assess your past performance. Find out the worst cases where you have been comfortable incurring losses. There are several factors that could affect your risk tolerance capacity. For instance, if you have high possibilities of earning increased income in the near future, this will influence how much you can stomach. Also, if you are looking to take advantage of future securities such as a pension, then your risk tolerance rate will also be high. Generally, you will be ready to face huge risks when you are sure that you have other assets that can earn you additional income. The forms of risk tolerance are detailed as follows.

Aggressive Risk Tolerance

Traders who have profound experience in day trading would find it easy to face the risk of investing in highly volatile securities. This is influenced by the fact that they are well informed about market trends. With their expertise, they can easily predict the next trend of a particular security. Often, they can tolerate any changes in the market. On a good day, they maximize returns with the greatest risks. This is what aggressive risk tolerance is all about.

Moderate Risk Tolerance

Moderate traders will accept some risks but will shy away from securities that are too risky. In this case, they will go for markets which are less volatile. Their main aim is to minimize the possible risks that they are likely to face.

Conservative Risk Tolerance

Conservative traders are quite different from aggressive and moderate traders. Just as the name suggests, these investors will try their best to minimize risks at all costs. Traders that fall into this category are mostly retirees.

From the information provided, where do you lie? How risk tolerant are you? You should realize that your tolerance capacity will change with time as you will learn how to cope with losses. However, it is vital that you know what works best for you right from the get-go. The significance of this is that you will prevent yourself from giving up each time you incur losses that you never expected. Knowing

your risk tolerance is part of your trading foundation
which will confirm that you grow to become a
successful trader.

Chapter 3

Day Trading Tools

Day Trading prediction techniques

There are certain Day trading techniques or tools (as we like to call them) that you can utilize to forecast the pattern that the stocks will follow.

Candlesticks

These are the most widely used techniques of prediction.

Fibonacci numbers

The mathematical technique that is utilized to predict stocks is the Fibonacci technique. Once you know how a Fibonacci series works, you will find it easy to comprehend. Your securities and stocks will follow a Fibonacci pattern and this will help you identify where it will stop next. Using this knowledge, you can choose either to stay or withdraw.

Rebate trading

Rebate trading is a popular technique. In this technique, you will be trading via an electronic communication network. These ECNs have been constructed to help people invest their money wit ease. Once everybody's money is pooled together, the ECN will invest it in the stock market. It is found to be safe and helpful.

Range trading

Range trading is another good prediction technique. It is necessary to have boundaries and work within a range. To do this you will have to set limits to your investments. You can choose your limits.

Price action

In price action technique we make predictions by looking at the current prices. The trader makes some assumptions. If he thinks that those prices are falling and will continue to fall, he won't invest in them. If he feels those prices are rising and will continue to rise, he will not invest in it. This is an extremely safe approach and works only if one pays close attention to the trends.

Contrarian trading

Contrarian trading means doing the opposite of what the crowd is doing. Here, you buy stocks when people are selling them and sell stocks when people are buying them. This risk usually pays off but you need to know when to carry it out.

News forecasts

You should keep track of the news articles to be aware of the changes that are occurring in the company. If the share value is going up the company announces profits and dividends. On the other hand, if the share value will go down the company announces that it has undergone a loss and the steps it will take to minimize the effect of the loss or how they will rebuild. You need to work with this knowledge.

Software

There are different kinds of software that will help you with your stock investments. You have to see which works best for you. They help you read and predict the trends. This software can be installed by you on your own or with the help of a friend or broker.

The other essentials tools are a good computer or laptop, good telephone connection and a fast Internet connection.

Importance of using these day trading tools:

These are the different prediction techniques that you must take into account to be successful in day trading. You can choose any of these day trading tools to help you in your venture. In today's world, you cannot expect to succeed without the help of these tools. You require technology to assist you in your trades.

Some of the benefits of these tools are:

● Gives you an edge over other investors in the market.

● Will help you save time and energy

● Will help in the formation an advantageous strategy and increase your chances of being successful.

How Fibonacci numbers can help you trade better:

1.   Some academics agree that Fibonacci numbers are powerful in financial markets.

2.   These numbers offer a framework for evaluating price action

3.   These numbers are watched by traders and provide key horizontal price levels.

4.   These price levels tend to bring higher levels or more volume and thus, can lead to a promising trade setup.

Chapter 4 Fundamental Analysis

Fundamental Analysis

In order to successfully trade in the forex market, one of the most important things you are going to need to learn is to determine a reliable way to tell a potentially profitable trade from one that is likely to fizzle out or, even worse, cost you money. This is where proper analysis comes into play either through technical analysis (outlined below) or via fundamental analysis. Fundamental analysis is used more frequently by new traders, while technical analysis has experienced something of a renaissance in popularity over the past decade or so. While both are useful when it comes to finding the information you are looking for, they go about determining just what that information is in different ways. Fundamental analysis is primarily concerned with looking at the big picture, which often means that it will take longer to perform than its counterpart.

Additionally, its information comes from external sources which means you may need to wait for additional information to become available though it will typically end up being easier to digest than the information required to utilize technical analysis effectively. Broadly, fundamental analysis makes it easier for you to glimpse the likely future of the forex market based on a wide variety of different variables including publicized changes to the monetary policy of the countries you are interested in. The end goal is to track down enough information to allow you to find an undervalued currency pair that the market has not adjusted to.

Determine the baseline: When it comes to considering the fundamental aspects of a currency pair, you will first want to consider the baseline that these currencies typically return to time after time when compared to the other currency pairs that are commonly traded. This will make it easier to determine when the right time to make a move is likely to be as you will then be more easily able to pinpoint changes that occur to the pair that make them warrant additional consideration.

In order to determine this baseline, the first thing you will need to consider is any changes to the related macroeconomic policy that affects each based on historical data. In these instances, past behavior is one of the most reliable indicators when it comes to determining likely future events. Once you are aware of the relevant historical context you will then need to consider the current phase that the currency is in and how likely it is to remain in the phase in question as opposed to moving on to the next.

Each currency regularly goes through 6 distinct phases, the first of which is the boom phase which can be identified via low volatility and large amounts of liquidity. At the opposite end of the spectrum is the bust phase which can be identified by the opposite, mainly low amounts of liquidity and high amounts of volatility. The other phases are post-bust and pre-bust and post-boom and pre-boom which means that one of the major phases is either on its way in or on its way out. Determining the proper phase is crucial when it comes to ensuring that you are on the right track when it comes to finding a trading pair that is likely to be profitable in the long-term.

In order to determine the current phase, the easiest way to go about doing so is by looking at the current number of defaults along with bank loans as well as the accumulated reserve levels of the related currencies. If the numbers are low then a boom phase is likely on its way or possibly in full swing already. If the current numbers have already overstayed their welcome then you can be confident that a post-boom phase is likely to start at any time. Alternatively, if the numbers in question are higher than the baseline you have already established then you know that the currency is likely either due for a bust phase or is already underway.

Money can be made regardless of the current phase as long as you can capitalize on it before the market catches up as it is typically fairly slow moving.

Worldwide considerations: After you have an understanding of the baseline the currency pairs you are working with tend to remain at, the next thing you will want to do is to determine is what the related global economic conditions are likely to be and how they are going to affect your trading pair. In order for this to be effective, you are going to want to look beyond the obvious signals and dig deep to find the indicators that are surely going to make waves after they become public knowledge. One of the best ways to go about doing so is to looking into emerging technologies in the related countries as they can easily turn entire economies on their heads in a relatively short period of time.

Technological indicators are a great way to use a boom phase to its full advantage as by getting in on the ground floor you can ride the wave for as long as it takes for that technology to become a full- fledged part of the mainstream. After it reaches the saturation point then you are going to want to be on the lookout for the bust phase as it will likely be right around the corner. If you feel as though the countries related to the currencies in question will soon be in a post-bust or post-boom phase then you will want to think twice about moving into speculative markets as the drop off is sure to be coming and it can be difficult to determine exactly when it will rear its ugly head.

If you feel confident that a phase shift is on the horizon but you don't know when it will be exactly then you are going to want to stick with smaller leverage points than you would during the other phases to ensure that they will pay out before the change occurs. On the other hand, if a phase is just starting then you will want to go ahead and make riskier trades as the time concerns aren't going to come into play which means extra caution is less warranted.

Global implications: While regional concerns are a good place to start, it is also important to take a macro view of the market as a whole, as global currency policies are almost always likely to play a part in the proceedings. While it might be difficult to determine where you should start, at first, all you really need to do is to apply the same level of analysis that you have performed on the micro level, just on a larger scale. The best place to start is generally going to be with the interest rates of the major players on the world stage include the Federal Reserve, the European Central Bank, th Bank of England and the Bank of Japan.

You will also need to be aware of any policy biases or legal mandates that are currently making the rounds in order to ensure that you don't end up getting blindsided from these sources when it comes time for you to make your move. While this will certainly be time consuming work, understanding the market from all sides will make it easier to determine new emerging markets when specific areas are fat with supply growth and what the expectations regarding interest rate changes or market volatility are soon going to be.

Understand the past: After you have a clear idea of what the current state of the worldwide economy is looking like, along with the specifics regarding the currency pairs you are interested in trading, then the next thing you will need to do is look to the past so that you can be prepared for history to repeat itself. This level of understanding will make it easier for you to understand the current strength of your respective currencies while also allowing you to more accurately determine the length of time you can expect the current phase to continue.

In order to capitalize on this knowledge in the most effective way possible, you are going to want to attempt to jump onto trades when one of the currencies is entering a post-bust phase while the other is in the midst of a post-boom phase. When this occurs, credit channels will not yet be exhausted and you will be able to take advantage of the greatest amount of risk possible when compared to any other market state.

Be aware of volatility: Being aware of the current level of volatility is crucial when it comes to ensuring that the investments you are making are likely to actually pay out in your favor. This is relatively easy to do, all you need to do is to pay attention to the stock markets most closely related to the currencies you favor.

This is because the forex market tends to be more stable, the more stable the stock market is because the lower the perceived overall risk is, the lower the amount of perceived risk that can make its way to the forex market.

Remember, the closer to the peak of the boom phase you currently find yourself, the lower interest rates, default rates, and volatility will be which means it is the best time to increase your level of risk. Alternately, the closer you find yourself to the bust phase, the higher the overall level of volatility, default and interest rates are going to be.

Decide on the best currency pairs: With a good idea of where the market currently is and how long it is likely to stay there, all that you have left to do is determine the most effective currency pairs to actually sell. To do this you must first consider any gap between the 2 currencies when it comes to interest rates. You need to have a clear understanding of where each of the pair are currently and how likely they are going to remain close together and with a proper distribution between them.

To find this information you are going to want to start by looking at the difference in the output gap as well as related unemployment statistics. When capacity constraints increase, while at the same time unemployment decreases, this shortage will lead to an inflated economy, which in turn, will cause interest rates will rise until the economy begins to cool. Charting this information will allow you to accurately determine the likely interest rate movement from the pair in question.

Additionally, you will want to consider the payment balance of the nations related to the currencies in question. The healthier the debt to capital ratio, the stronger the related currency is likely to remain in times of crisis. To determine this amount, you are going to want to consider the capital as well as the current account and the general situation of each. This will help you to determine if the position the nation in question is holding is due to asset sales or bank deposits or other, long term potential developments including things like an accumulation of reserves or foreign investment.

Economic indicators to watch

When it comes to major economic indicators, the list is a fairly short one. Unfortunately, if you hope to stay competitive in the forex market then you are going to need to keep up with far more than just the basics. This is easier said than done, however, as there are a huge variety of economic surveys and other relevant indicators that can be used to predict numerous types of trends before they happen. While the entire list is too massive to include in its entirety, the options listed below will get you started on the right track.

This is because, rather than simply present the reader with raw data, it instead uses a tone that is much more conversational as it describes the various regional goings on of the various members of the United States Federal banking districts. This allows traders to determine how the Fed comes t various conclusions in various circumstances which, in turn, can be useful later on when it comes to making bets on how the currency will move in the future. This economic indicator is published prior to each Federal Open Market Committee Meeting, which works out to be 8 times per year.

While the beige book does not typically crate that much of a commotion as it doesn't present anything strictly new, instead, it helps to point knowledgeable traders in the likely direction that things are going to be moving in the future. For example, if the overall tone of a beige book indicates a growing worry about inflation, then you might be able to start making preliminary plans related to a decrease in the current USD interest rate.

Consumer price index: A consumer price index is a sort of benchmark for a specific country's economy and its current level of inflation. It utilizes a basket approach as it attempts to compare a steady base of products that don't change much from year to year. These products include many common items including toiletries and other common groceries in addition to everyday services like the price of a haircut or an oil change.

These numbers tend to be broken down into a handful of figures, the first of which is broken down into two categories known as the Urban Wage Earners and the Clerical Workers. The second category is known as Urban Consumers. The consumer price index for a given set of urban consumers is often tracked quite closely as it varies dramatically throughout the year. In the US, the current percentage is shown in comparison to the year 1982 so changes can only be determined based on previous index levels. Numbers are then shown via a run rate of grown to show traders what they can expect from inflation as well.

Meanwhile, the chain-weighted consumer price index often sees a major push when it comes to relevancy. This index provides a numerical visualization of customer purchasing patterns when compared to other indexes. As an example, only the chain weighted index notes things like when the public shifts from one brand to another based on things like price increases.

In addition to major economic indicators like these, the consumer price index is often viewed by many trades as the final say when it comes to the up to date financial situation of a given country. It is released once per month and when it is you can count on serious movement for any related currency pairs.

Durable Goods Report: This report is released monthly and provides valuable updates when it comes to the amount of manufacturing that is being done in a given country when it comes to durable goods. A durable good is any type of capital good that has an average lifespan of more than three years. Nearly 100 different industries fall under this report's purview including things like cars, semiconductors and even wind turbines. The figures for a given country will be provided in the currency of that company along with a percentage of change for the month over month numbers. Three months of revisions are also included in every report. Data from this report is one of the 10 core components of the US Conference Board Leading Index which is used to divine future movement i the global market.

When it comes to reading these reports it is vital that you always remember that the numbers that are publicly reported often do not include transportation goods or items created by the defense sector as they tend to be volatile enough to skew things dramatically one way or the other. Thus, if you want the full story on a given country you will need to do your due diligence and sniff these numbers out for yourself.

Generally speaking, the durable goods report is an excellent way for savvy traders to get a viable overview of business demand in specific countries. This is the case because these types of capital goods tend to require a larger overall investment which, in turn, shows that business owners and consumers are both acting with greater confidence than they would be if the economy was not moving in a positive direction.

Based on the results you find you may also find it especially useful to consider topics like the variation that occurs when it comes to inventory and shipment ratios over a prolonged period of time in addition to the growth rate of shipments and related inventories. Taken together, these should provide a much clearer picture of whether or not supply is exceeding demand or vice versa. As these types of goods often take far longer to be created than more transient goods, the durable goods report can also be an excellent way to get an early read on the expected earnings increases for the future month as an influx of orders in one month is a good sign that additional growth will be forthcoming.

Employment cost index: The employment cost index is a useful economic indicator that is released four times per year. It focuses on the amount that businesses in a given country pay for each employee, on average, as well as how much that has changed over the proceeding quarter. This report looks at things like employee benefits, hourly wages, bonuses and any relevant employee premiums for every industry besides government and farm labor as these would skew the numbers at either end of the spectrum.

This data is then broken down on an industry by industry basis before being split even further based on whether or not the industry is unionized. This information tends to also be broken down industry by industry which makes it especially useful to traders who are looking for early indicators when it comes to determining potential signs of inflation. This is due to the fact that the cost for compensating employees is the greatest cost almost any industry faces and they tend to be presented in terms of the cost to the company in relation to the amount of profit that is generated when it comes to particular goods and services that are being generated.

Based on its overall outlook, the employee cost index can actually be enough to change the direction of a specific currency completely. This will occur if the actual report comes back in such a way that it is dramatically different from what all estimates expected. This is because these types of compensation costs are almost always passed off onto consumers which leads to further GDP projection reductions when it is left untreated in the long-term. This is also one of several indicators that is useful when it comes to determining a country's overall assumed level of productivity. If productivity grows at a slower rate than the rate at which compensation costs are increasing, then the valuation of the related currency is going to decrease and vice versa.

Focus on interest rates: After you have a clear idea of the market as a whole and major currencies specifically, you are going to want to focus on what many traders in the forex market focus on the most, the difference in interest rates between various currencies. This is a crucial step if you hope to form an accurate opinion on the strengths of various relevant central banks, which in turn factors into an accurate qualitative analysis of the situation as a whole.

To form a clearer picture in this regard you are going to want to consider the unemployment statistics of both countries as well as the gap in output that each has. If the economy is increasing, while at the same time, available labor is decreasing, then this will eventually lead to inflation and overall higher rates. This, in turn, will lead to higher rates from the central bank which will keep them there until the economy starts heading in the other direction. Keeping an eye on these trends will leave you with a clear idea of what your qualitative analysis has revealed.

Take stock of each country's external position: When it comes to getting the proper feel for a currency or currency pair it is important to keep in mind how healthy their balance of payments currently is. If one of the countries in question has a position that is generally considered to be maintained via asset sales and bank deposits, which can dry up or change direction relatively quickly, then that is less reassuring than a country with long term commitments such as reserve accumulation or foreign direct investment.

Chapter 5 Technical Analysis

When working with technical analysis you are always going to want to remember that it functions

because of the belief that the way the price of a given trade has moved in the past is going to be an equally reliable metric for determining what it is likely to do again in the future. Regardless of which market you choose to focus on, you'll find that there is always more technical data available than you will ever be able to realistically parse without quite a significant amount of help. Luckily, you won't be sifting through the data all on your own, and you will have numerous technical tools including things such as charts, trends, and indicators to help you push your success rates to new heights.

While some of the methods you will be asked to apply might seem arcane at first, the fact of the matter is that all you are essentially doing is looking to determine future trends along with their relative strengths. This, in turn, is crucial to your long-term success and will make each of your trades more reliable practically every single time.

Understand core assumptions: Technical analysis is all about measuring the relative value of a particular trade or underlying asset by using available tools to find otherwise invisible patterns that, ideally, few other people have currently noticed. When it comes to using technical analysis properly you are going to always need to assume three things are true. First and foremost, the market ultimately discounts everything; second, trends will always be an adequate predictor of price and third, history is bound to repeat itself when given enough time to do so.

Technical analysis believes that the current price of the underlying asset in question is the only metric that matters when it comes to looking into the current state of things outside of the market, specifically because everything else is already automatically factored in when the current price is set as it is. As such, to accurately use this type of analysis all you need to know is the current price of the potential trade in question as well as the greater economic climate as a whole.

Understanding trend: To use technical analysis properly it is important to understand how trends work and how best to analyze them. In forex, a trend is any noticeable grouping of pricing data that points in either a negative or positive direction which indicates the direction the market will likely move in a predetermined period of time. Trends that are very easy to pick out are said to be strong which those that are more difficult to see are said to be weak.

While strong trends speak for themselves, it is important to be cautious around weak trends as it can be easy to mistake random market movement for a weak trend that doesn't exist. This is more difficult than it might initially seem as forex prices have been known to clump together in a suspicious fashion or to move around erratically in ways that trends typically signify. In order to minimize the likelihood of misidentifying a trend, the best thing to do is to focus on identifying the highest highs along with the lowest lows and discounting those data points in the middle. Remember, every data point doesn't need to line up perfectly to prove the existence of a specific trend when it comes to technical analysis majority rules.

Positive trends, also known as uptrends, and negative trends, also known as reversals, aren't the only types of trend that you need to be on the lookout for. Horizontal trends also exist and they are the definition of middle of the road. Specifically, a trend is said to be horizontal when all the moves that it makes are negated thanks to a series of opposite and equal moves in the other direction.

Trends can be of any length and the longer a trend is the stronger it is. If you come across a trend that seems to cut off shortly, it is important to look at the underlying price movement over a larger period of time to ensure that you just aren't missing the forest for the trees. The best way to ensure that you have accurately determined the type of trend you are looking at is to make it a habit to consult charts that cover both short and longer time spans as well.

Once you have properly consulted your charts, you will then want to generate a trendline as a means of determining if your assumptions are correct. For uptrends, you will need to connect the points of all the lowest prices over the given timeframe which a negative trend will see you connecting the points of the highest prices on the timeframe. If the trendline ultimately ends up above nearly all of the data points then it is a line of resistance, which is the point that price is likely to start receiving pushback when it is climbing. If the line is below most of the data points then it is the support line which means the price is unlikely to drop below it. This will not indicate how long a given trend is likely to continue, just where it is likely to end up when it peters out.

Finally, once you have come across a specific trend you will need to determine the channel it is a part of which is crucial when it comes to determining the right time to act on the information you have chosen. To do so, you will need to first determine both the price floor as well as the price ceiling of the currency in question. This will make it easier for you to determine if the trend is neutral, negative or positive as it should clearly be one of the 3. You will then want to trace what is known as a channel between the pair of lines for as long as it takes for the price to break through it. The breaking point is going to be your time to make a move as it indicates the period when significant negative or positive movement is going to occur.

Indicators to watch

Moving average convergence divergence indicator: The moving average convergence divergence (MACD) indicator is a type of oscillating indicator that generally moves between the centerline and zero. If the MACD value is high, then this indicates the related stock is close to being overbought an if the value is low then the stock is in danger of being oversold.

MACD charts are generally based on a combination of multiple exponential moving averages (EMAs). These averages can be based on any timeframe, though the most common is the 12-26-9 chart. This chart is typically broken into multiple parts, the first of which is the 26-day and 12-day chart. Using an EMA that is slower or fast allows you to more accurately gauge the current momentum level for the trend you are currently keeping an eye on.

If the 12-day EMA, the fast of the pair, ends up being above the 26-day EMA then you can safel assume that the underlying stock is on an uptrend while the reverse will also be the case. If the 12-day EMA increases at a rate that is greater than the 26-day EMA then the uptrend is generally going to be even more pronounced. IF the 12-day EMA starts to move closer to the 26-day then you ca accurately assume that it is slowing down which means the momentum of the trade is going to fade. This, in turn, means you should expect the uptrend to end shortly.

The MACD puts these EMAs to use by considering the difference between them and then plotting i out. If the 26-day and the 12-day end up being the same then the MACD will equal out to 0. If the 12 day ends up ends up at a higher point than the 26-day then the MACD will end up being positive otherwise, it will be negative. The larger the difference between them, the further the MACD lin will fall from zero if the result is negative, or from the center line if the result is positive.

While the MACD doesn't provide all that much more detail when compared to the standard movin average, its value increases dramatically when it is used in conjunction with the 9-day EMA as well. The 9-day EMA differs from the other EMAs in that it is based on the MACD line as opposed to th stock price. As a result, this EMA then smooths out the MACD line to make its results more usefu overall.

On certain occasions, you will also find a use for the MACD histogram which visualizes th difference between the MACD line and the 9-day EMA line. If the MACD line cross through the 9 day EMA line at a point higher than 0, then the upcoming trend is likely to be bearish, otherwise it is likely to be bullish. If the charted histogram generates a number of descending peaks, then this will be known as a negative divergence, while a positive divergence forms in the opposite way.

If a negative divergence occurs, then it is a strong sign

that any positive trends that are currently in place will be reversing sooner than later. This will remain true in all scenarios, even if the underlying stock price seems to be in the midst of a very strong positive trend. The same is true in the opposite sense for positive divergence and negative trends. These signals can become somewhat muddy when the price trades at the range for a prolonged period of time which is why it is important to always use multiple indicators to avoid seeing false signals.

Consolidation indicators: Consolidation is the term used in technical analysis as a means to describe the fact that the price of a given stock tends to stick to the same pattern, regardless of the trading level that you view it from. More practically speaking, consolidation can be thought of as the period of indecisiveness that is guaranteed to come to an end after the price moves outside the existing pattern. These types of consolidation are surprisingly common and can be found across any price chart at nearly any timeframe.

When they do appear, technical traders tend to use them as a means of finding levels of resistance and support so that they can ensure the buying and selling decisions they make are as informed as possible. These levels are generated by the underlying asset and the fact that it is likely to vary a predetermined amount over a given period of time. This means that once the price moves outside either the pre-existing resistance or support level, volatility will increase dramatically as a result.

This volatile period is when smart traders will jump in to make serious profits in a short period of time. Furthermore, many technical traders believe that the breakout does occur on the side of the resistance then the price is going to typically continue to move upward which means you would want to go long in response. However, if the breakout instead occurs so that it is on par with the existing support then it is likely that the price is going to continue to decrease which means you will want to take a short position instead.

Both pennants and flags are signs of retracements or deviations from the existing trend that eventually become visible in the short term if viewed in comparison to the existing trend. Retracements rarely lead to breakouts occurring in either direction, but the underlying asset likely won't be following the dominant trend in the first place so this shouldn't be much of an issue.

Chapter 6

Day Trading Forex

"The trend is your friend until the end when it bends."
– Ed Seykota

FOREX trading revolves around making money on the small fluctuations that happen every day o currency markets. FOREX markets are open twenty-four hours a day, are fairly resilient to news coverage for large effects in trading, and have a variety of currency pairs with different types of volatility. FOREX is not my first go to market when day trading, as I find the number of peopl trading FOREX produces a lot of noise on the exchange. It can be difficult to identify trends on thei way up or indeed on their way down due to the number of inexperienced traders that muddle the key data that is used to estimate what trades are good investments. My suggestion for all future traders is that you only explore

FOREX markets if you do not meet the capital requirements for the larger stoc exchanges.

Key Strategies

Momentum Trading

When I trade FOREX, I use one very simple strategy, momentum trading. This is very much the sam tactic that we use on the large stock exchanges and even on penny stocks. The difference with FOREX markets is in your ability to peer through the noise of the market and identify currency pairs that are actually appreciating. To find the ideal picks, you essentially rely on two pieces of relevant data, the volatility and volume of a currency pair. You need good measurements in each metric to make picks successfully. The problem with currency pairs is that often those with high volatility do not have the volume to support day traders, and those with high volume do not have the volatility to make enough profit for day traders. I have found that, in recent times, the best way to make money through FOREX is to make educated guesses about the long-term effects government policy may have on the relation between countries. For example, one of the key currency pairs that I have been trading recently is the US dollar/Peso. This currency pair has seen lots of volatility due to minor news stories from President Donald Trump, but these changes have not been enough to make a great deal of profit unless you got the timing exactly right, something that is hard to do on FOREX markets because they ar open twenty-four hours a day.

To make a great profit from FOREX, you will need to ride out long changes in a currency pair's value based on news and changes in governmental policy that will have long-lasting implications. This has always been true, but in recent times, it has become more difficult to discern what is going to make a policy difference in currency markets and what is merely a small change in currency pairs that will be normalized within just a few days. My suggestion going forward is to use FOREX market conservatively and trade on the upswings of dollar/foreign pairs. For example, focus on currency pairs that feature the dollar pegged against another currency from a well-known country that is going to decline due to recent policy decisions. This is why I am so invested in the Peso right now, and how I have been able to make a decent profit over the last several months in even modest jumps in the Peso's value. When the Peso is trading low, which it does at several times a month nowadays, you should purchase it, and wait for clear policy changes that will boost the value. I've sold some of my holdings based off of minor news stories and the impact that they have had, but in general, this is a long-term strategy for me. I will not be selling my holdings of the Mexican Peso, probably for two or more years, or at least until relations between the US and Mexico get better. This can seem quite antithetical to what it means to be a day trader, but from my own experience, it seems the best bets in FOREX work on the scale of months, not hours or days.

Pullback

I have a lot of friends that trade in various markets. Of all of them, I only know a few that trade on

FOREX exclusively. Of this small subset of traders, I only know one that can use the pullbac strategy successfully with any consistency. The pullback strategy is one of the most difficult to implement, and while it can be, in fact, used on stocks as well, it serves its highest chance of success on FOREX markets. The basic strategy is that a trader waits for a currency pair to drop in value bu believes that this decline is only temporary and that another rally will follow up shortly. The trader buys into a currency pair, believing that they missed the last opportunity to buy low but believing that the pullback they are experiencing now is only temporary. The logic is that investors are being scared off because they want to cash out their profits.

Meanwhile, other pullback investors will be jumping in to catch the next rally, thus promoting the next rally. For example, suppose that the currency pair USD/NZD was climbing upwards for severa months. There were occasional downturns, but in general, the pair was rising nicely. This would tell a trader that it is likely the pair will continue to rise in the future but that the current price to buy is too high to make a good amount of profit. A trader will then buy the currency pair the next time there is a rapid selloff, assuming the pair will continue to go upward after the selloff. This is a strategy that I've seen work, but have had little success using it myself. This is mainly due to lack of trying, and FOREX not being my main market where I trade. I would suggest invoking this strategy if you spen three or four months trading FOREX and notice an upward trend that has been consistent. The nex time there is a pullback in the value, that is the time to pick up the currency pair.

Chapter 7

Penny Stocks

Penny stocks are some of the most preferred types of stocks for day trading. Penny stocks refer to those that are valued at $5 or less. Although they are known as penny or cent stocks, they are hardly ever valued at such a low price.

Penny stocks came into the limelight when one Jordan Belfort converted his hundreds into millions by trading in these stocks. Although he did experience overnight riches, he later confessed to have controlled the market unlawfully.

But it is possible for a person to make money in the penny stock market through legal means. It takes patience and dedication for positive results to come through.

Penny stocks are exchanged over the counter, as they are not listed in the stock market. No big stock market entertains them given their low prices and extreme volatility. Penny stocks are not your average stocks and so, are dispensed through the pink sheet system.

You can buy the stocks by purchasing the sheets and trade with them. Authorized agents will have access to these stocks and can get them for you. You have to inform them in advance so that they can make arrangements for it.

Predicting penny stocks

As is with most other stocks, it will benefit you to predict the pattern of penny stocks. When you successfully predict whether a stock will rise or fall, you have the chance to safeguard your investment and also make the most of it.

We already looked at the different prediction methods that you can implement to understand the movement of a stock and you can apply the same techniques to your penny stocks as well. Apart from them, here are some more that you can put to practice.

Change in volume

If you spot any unusual change in the volume of the stock then you must investigate the cause. It is also a signal for you to invest in the particular stock, as it is sure to rise further in value. The volume needs to rise up drastically in order for any significant change to occur in it. You have to therefore keep track of all the stocks that you have in your possession and also book mark some that you wish to stock.

Flow of money

Next, look at the flow of money in the company. If a lot of money has flown into the company through funding then it is a good place to invest. You have to keep track of the news to see where the money has come from and how much it is. In general, it is possible for you to guess from the invested amount, how much would be a good bet for you to invest. Of course you need to perform the different technical and fundamental analysis. Without it, you would be taking a risk.

Market capture

Market capture or market share refers to the stock's overall presence in the market. You can look at how many shares of the company are being traded in the market. You must also call up the customer support team to enquire about the same. If the company's market share is large, then chances are it will do well. However, don't base your judgement on this one criterion alone. You have to conduct due research on the topic.

Name game

If the company in question is having its named mentioned in the media for one reason or the other, then it is probably going to do well. Many times, the news will be of a negative nature and yet, the company will receive publicity. So, regardless of what the news is about, if a company's name is being splashed all over the media, then chances are high that its stock will do well.

Product launch

If the penny stock company has launched something new then that can be reason for its stock prices to rise. If the product is launched on a grand scale then chances are high that the stock will do simply great. You have to be on the lookout for news of any new products that are being launched. Remember that penny stock companies might not be as big or opulent like regular companies, but they will have a large enough reach to remain in the news.

Anticipation

You have to capitalize on the power of anticipation. This means that you must not wait for the company to announce its results and buy the shares just before it does. As soon as the results are announced, a form of buying frenzy takes place. Many people don't even bother to check if the results are positive or negative and buy in bulk. You have to time your sales correctly during such times. When a lot of demand for the stock occurs, you have to wisely sell them in the market. So there is no point in waiting to see if the company is putting out a profit or a loss.

The final call will always be yours and you have to do your research on the topic first.

Chapter 8

Trading Strategies and Techniques

When it comes to trading, there are more strategies available than I can possibly put in one book. Par of the reason for this is because so many strategies can be used for different types of trading and investing. Another reason is that traders seem to be coming up with new forms of techniques all the time. However, I have chosen some of the most popular strategies that are used by day traders to outline here.

ABCD Pattern

This is a strategy that uses a specific pattern in order to help you find the exact time you should sell your stock. There are four parts to this pattern:

A - the initial high price of the stock.

B - the lowest price of the stock, which occurs when people start selling once they see the stock has hit A.

C - the establishment of the higher low. This is the point where people who follow the ABCD pattern will start the selling process of their stock.

D - the highest profitable point. This is the point the stock rises to, which gives the day trader a large profit.

This strategy is known to not only be a bit tricky, but also risky. This is because the trader has to sell at the specified point of C, which is when the stock starts to rise in price after reaching point B. O course, the biggest risk is that the stock falls below point B *after* the trader sells at point C. This would mean that the trader receives a bigger loss than anyone who sold right after point A. However, the hope is that the price of the stock rises past point A, which gives the trader a large profit.

The ABCD pattern I explained above is just one of the patterns that you will see as a trader. Som patterns show point A to be the lowest price and point B to be the stock's highest price. However, the trader still sells at point C and hopes to reach point D to gain the best profit.

Bull Flag Momentum

This strategy received its bull flag name because the trend lines resemble a flagpole. After the stock reaches a high price, it has a short-term down trend. However, it quickly spikes up before spiking back down another time. This trend repeats one more time and leaves a pattern where the high prices and the low prices are parallel to each other. However, the pattern ends when the price spikes back up, exceeding the previous highest price. This is when traders begin to sell in hopes of making the best profit.

The trick to catching the bull flag strategy is that you look for the pattern where the high and low prices are parallel to each other, yet they are either slowly moving up or down the chart. Both of these directions signal that the stock can quickly spike up in price and exceed its previous high price.

Volume Weighted Average Price (VWAP) Trading

VWAP trading takes the price and volume of a stock to give you an average price. It is known as a trading benchmark, and will give traders an idea of the trend and security of the stock. Like most trading strategies, the VWAP can be used with specific software that will perform the algorithms for each step. However, it is possible to calculate the VWAP yourself.

This type of strategy can be used by various investors and traders. For example, both day traders and buy-and-hold investors can use the VWAP technique. However, it is more popular with short-term trades. This strategy will start new at the beginning of the day and give you a running total at the end of the day. This is one of the reasons buy-and-hold investors use this strategy, as it allows them to analyze the stock.

Electronic Communication Network (ECN) and Level II

This type of strategy involves watching the trades in real time. It is similar to going to a horse race and watching the race to see if you are going to win or lose your money. The ECN is an automated system where traders from all over can trade with you. Day traders who take on the business by themselves, without the help of a broker, usually use the ECN strategy because it's fairly easy to navigate and is known to take out any middleman. This is a benefit as it takes away any brokerage fees and can make trades more profitable because it is known to save time. On top of this, the ECN allows for after-market trading, which means you can trade after the regular trading hours of the day.

There are several charts available that will allow you to see the price changes of stocks throughout the day. All of the charts will allow you to compare the opening price to the closing price. On top of this, the charts will also allow you to see the various price changes in the stock during the day.

1. Candlestick Charts

Most day traders use candlestick charts as they find them essential for the business. These charts are helpful because they will display specific security prices on a daily basis. Once you learn how to analyze candlestick charts, you will be able to tell when the highest and lowest prices for any of your stocks will be, which will help you increase your profits. Furthermore, you will be able to learn where the stock sits at both opening and closing that day. If the candlestick has a red or black color, then the closing price of the stock is lower than the opening price. If the candlestick has a green or white color, then you know that the closing price is higher than the opening price. You can also analyze more about the stock through the shadow of the candlestick. The shadow will tell you what the prices were throughout the stock's day. You can then take this analysis and compare it to the opening and closing prices.

2.   Line Charts

Line charts are another popular chart type that day traders use often. While these charts give you the same information as candlestick charts, they will only work if you have the specified charting software. However, this is becoming more typical with any type of chart you want to use. This is because the charting software that is on the market today will allow you to develop the charts you want to use and include all the information you need in order to analyze the stocks on a daily basis.

3.   Bar Charts

Many day traders like to use bar charts because they are some of the easiest charts to read. There are four main prices that you will find if you use bar charts. The first one is the opening price. The second price is the highest price and the third is the lowest price of the day. The final price you will see through the chart is the closing price. Through these four prices, you can start to analyze what the day-to-day process is for any stock you are interested in.

Spread Trading

Spread trading, also known as scalping, is defined as trading securities over a period of seconds to minutes. The reason this type of technique has become popular is because traders feel that they can catch stocks easier when they follow small growths over large increments. The number of transactions day traders go through can vary from a dozen to over 200 within a day. Traders make so many transactions because they will sell the stock as soon as it will give them a profit.

This type of technique is known to be relatively safe, which is another reason why so many traders consider themselves spread traders. Traders who follow this technique are often considered to be market makers, as they help maintain the liquidity of the market.

If you are thinking about looking more into this strategy, then you will want to note the following three points:

Low Profits Comes from Large Volume

Traders who use the spread trading technique state this strategy is not useful for people who want to move large volumes of shares at one time. They will not be able to make the money they want by using this strategy as large volumes give low profits. This happens because the profit margin, which is the measure of profitability, neglects the large volume investor. Therefore, the best type of traders for spread trading are the ones who are interested in moving small volumes.

You Will Have a Lower Risk if You Lower Your Exposure

Traders who take on the technique of scalping will limit their risk of loss because they don't hang onto their stocks for a long period of time. In fact, most traders will hold on to the majority of their shares for only a few minutes, very rarely reaching an hour.

Smaller Moves are Easier

I have already stated that you want to move small volumes in order to gain the best benefits as a spread trader. People who follow this technique become pros at finding the small moves with the small spreads that tend to happen frequently throughout the day. The reason spread traders focus on small moves is not only because they are easier to handle using this technique but also because this is where they will find their best profits.

Trend Following

Traders refer to trend following as trading stocks because of their trends over their market value. This type of technique is not only used in day trading, but in all types of stock market transactions. How long you will follow the trend before you decide to take a stock because of its trend depends on what type of trading you are doing. In day trading, you won't spend more than a couple of hours on the trend. However, if you are into swing trading, you might analyze the trend for a few days to a couple of weeks.

Many traders like to take part in this technique because they feel that they know what the stock is going to do. Because you have watched for a trend to develop and then analyzed the trend to make sure it's a purchase you would like to make, your confidence about what the stock will do in the future increases. On top of this, many traders feel that they are more likely to succeed in making a profit because they can watch for stocks that will give you capital instead of loss.

At the same time, you always want to pay attention to all the factors that affect the trend of a stock. The factors you should consider if you decide to use trend following are:

Money Management

Money management is one consideration, as if you have too much money, then you are at a risk of losing more money than you should. However, if you don't have enough money, you are unlikely to reap the benefits of that trade. When you look at money management, you pay a lot of attention to your risk, which will let you know how much money you should put into that stock.

Price

The most important factor you will want to pay attention to is the price of the stock. While day traders pay attention to price variations of the stock, the most important price to look at is the actual price of the stock in the moment. It is the actual price that will tell you whether you should invest in the stock or hold off.

Diversity

Diversity is a word that you will often see in the stock market. This refers to the different types of stocks that you have in your portfolio. This is also a term that you will find some traders following while some traders feel it's a waste of time. While it is controversial, there are many benefits of diversity, especially for traders and serious investors. On top of this, when you use diversity, you are able to follow trends better, as it is an important factor of trend following.

Risk

Another factor to consider is the amount of risk that comes with the trend. While you can never get rid of *all* the risk in trading, you want to limit it as much as possible. If you find you are looking at a trend that is high in risk, you may want to pick a different stock, especially as a day trader. However, there are traders who like stocks with higher risk. How much risk you are willing to take on in a stock is a personal preference. However, most experienced day traders say that if you truly want to be successful, you will limit your risk as much as possible.

Rules

Finally, you will always want to follow the rules. Not only follow the rules of day trading, but you will also want to follow the rules you have created for yourself. One reason for this is it helps you remain consistent in your trading, which will help increase your success rate. Another reason is because your rules will help you become systematic when you are choosing your stocks.

News Playing

This is a technique day trader use when they follow the news of the stock market. When most people think of the stock market, they imagine a person reading the newspaper to see how the price of stocks is doing that day. This is similar to news playing, however, most day traders pay attention to several sources of information. You can get the news information from any online communities you join, news outlets, or any other reports which are easily found online.

One of the most important factors when following the news playing technique is to make sure you keep your emotions in check. Experienced traders know well how emotions can affect your decisions when trading. They also know how this can cause a trader to lose a lot of money. One of the most popular historic examples of how emotions can affect the stock market is the stock market crash of 1929. This is the event that helped launch the United States into the Great Depression, which laste throughout the 1930s. One of the reasons the crash occurred was because of all the investors who decided to quickly sell their stocks because they saw prices dropping. They started to get anxious over the money they would lose if they didn't sell. On top of that, they started to worry about the stock market in general because the prices were becoming so low. Emotions were running high on Wall Street right before the stock market crash, which did not help the situation at all. In fact, many historians state that if people would have kept their stocks instead of selling them, America would have never seen such a horrible depression in its economy. As stated before, when stocks sell, the price declines. Therefore, the more people who sell, the more the price will drop. Because the price of stocks kept dropping, more people started to sell. Eventually, this led to the stock market crash.

It is always a good thing to make sure you are thinking

logically when you are making decisions in the stock market. If you find yourself thinking illogically, you are putting too much emotion into your decision. One of the best things to do when this happens is simply to take a break or pick a stock that you don't feel too much emotion towards. It's also important to remember that day trading isn't for everyone. If you are naturally a person with strong emotions, you might want to look at different trading or investing methods.

You also want to make sure that you continue to do your research. Once you see a news report, you want to look into how this news is affecting the stock. For example, if you read that CVS Pharmac donated thousands of dollars to a struggling community, you might find their stock prices increasing. The news can easily affect who buys and sells a company's stocks, as investors want to purchase stocks from companies they believe will be successful and are proud to own a share of. Therefore, the price of the stock will go up, but the value might also increase.

Of course, there is always negative news which can also affect stocks. If you find that you hold a stock in a company and you see a negative news article about them, you will probably want to sell your stock as quickly as possible because this will allow you to sell with less loss.

Fading

Not a lot of traders take part in fading because it is known to be one of the riskier strategies. Unless you have a good amount of experience in trading, it is best that you don't participate in fading, as it is considered a more advanced technique in the business. The basis of short selling is that the trader speculates on the stock's decline. Speculation means that the trader makes the transaction when the risk of losing capital is high because the trader expects that there will be a benefit or some type of gain from the trade.

Fading doesn't follow the trends of the market. They buy when the price of the stock is low and sell when the price is high. They often buy a stock when they feel the market has overreacted over recent news. One of the benefits is that there is little analysis that needs to be done before buying or selling.

Stop-Loss Trading

This type of strategy involves making a deal with your broker to sell a stock once it reaches a certain price. This is a popular strategy, in fact most experienced traders say you should use stop-loss trading because it gives you security in your business. This happens because you can decide to say that you will sell the stock when it is 13% below your purchasing price.

This type of strategy isn't always used to for day trading because sometimes the stock won't reach the percentage you set. Therefore, you continue to hold the stock and don't sell it at the end of the day.

Range Trading

Range trading is often compared to trend following, however they are different techniques. When you use range trading, you will watch a stock over a certain period of time. Like other techniques, the increase and decline of prices will present a pattern which is noticeable to the trader. The trader will watch the prices until they see a breakout in the pattern. A breakout is when the price dramatically inflates. The opposite of this, a breakdown, is when the price dramatically declines from its pattern. Once this happens, traders feel that this pattern will continue for some time.

In order to reduce risks when it comes to this strategy, traders will often set high and low limits. This means that once they have viewed where the stock's pattern is sitting for a couple of hours, they will set the highest and lowest price they will buy or sell. Then, once the breakout or breakdown occurs, the trader will take the step and buy or sell the stock.

Chapter 9

Introduction To Charts

A chart is a graphical representation of the asset prices over a period. It exhibits properties like price point, price scale and time scale. The day trader can find the price scale on the chart's right side. The scale goes from lowest to highest from top to bottom. Although it is such a simple concept, the price scale can have a complicated structure.

A linear price structure means that the space between the price points is of equal amount. If the difference between the first and second price points is 10, it will be the same for all price points. A logarithmic price structure has distances between two price points at equal percentage change. This means that if the price change is 25%, it will be the same for all the price points.

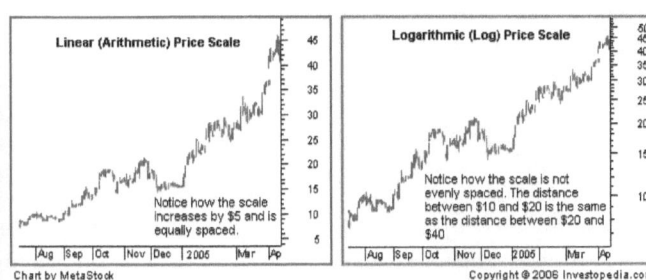

The time scale is a date or time range located at the
bottom of the chart. If he opts for a shorter timeframe,
the day trader can expect a more detailed chart with
each data point showing the asset's closing price.
Some charts can also show the open, high, low and
close prices.

An intraday chart can show price movements within a
particular period in one trading session. A day trader
can expect to see a time scale as short as five minutes.
A daily chart can have a series of price actions with a
trading session represented by one point, which can be

the open, high, low or close price.

Types of Chart

Traders and investors use four kinds of chart - line, bar, candlestick and point and figure charts. A line chart shows the close prices, connected by a line, over a period. It offers no other information.

A bar chart is an expansion of a line chart. It adds other information like the low and high prices with the close price for each data point. Usually, a dash on the left side illustrates the open price while a dash on the right illustrates the close price. A black bar represents a higher close price than the open price. A red bar represents a higher open price than the close price.

A candlestick chart shows a thin vertical line to illustrate the trading range of the period. It has a wide bar to show the difference between the open and close prices. Candlesticks use colors to explain what occurred during the trading period. However, there is no standard on the use of colors so the day trader has to find out the meaning of each color used by the chart site.

The point and figure chart is not popular. However, the first technical traders used it. The point and figure chart shows the price actions without the insignificant price movements that usually distort the price trends. It aims to neutralize the skewing effect.

Chart Patterns

A chart pattern is a formation on a chart, which suggests a future price action or triggers a trading signal. A chartist uses it to determine present trends and trend reversals to create a trading signal. Theoretically, a chart pattern signals a particular high probability price action. It must be clear, however, that it cannot determine a future price movement with 100% certainty.

A chart pattern can be a continuation or a reversal. A continuation pattern suggests that the prevailing trend will continue while a reversal pattern signals that a change in trend will occur.

Head and Shoulders

The head and shoulders pattern is popular and reliable. It suggests a trend reversal when formed. The head and shoulders top (left figure) signals the end of an upward trend. On the other hand, the head and shoulders down (right figure) suggest an end of the downtrend.

Cup and Handle

A cup and handle chart confirms a continuation of a bullish pattern. It usually shows a short pause but continues its uptrend upon confirmation of the pattern.

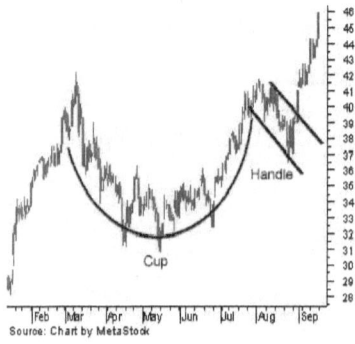

Double Tops and Bottoms

Both the double tops pattern and the double bottoms pattern signal a trend reversal. The pattern becomes visible when the price touches the support or resistance points twice without breaking through. It signals intermediate and long-term reversals.

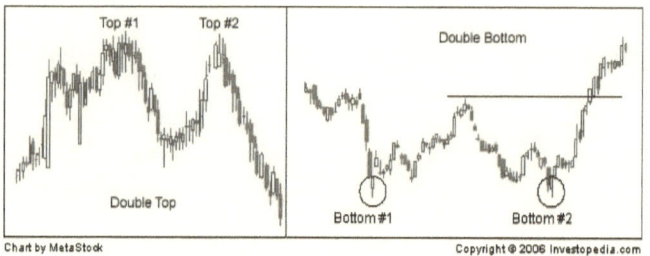

Flag and Pennant

The flag and pennant are two short-term continuation patterns formed during a sharp price action followed by a sideways movement. Another sharp price action completes the patterns. These two chart patterns develop up to three weeks.

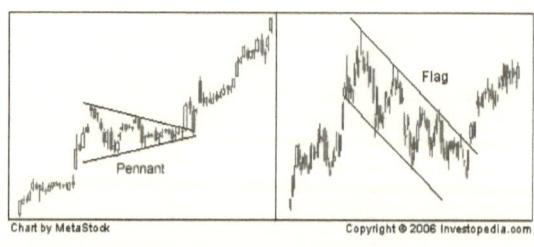

The midsection of the pennant chart pattern has converging trend lines while the midsection of the flag pattern has a channel pattern.

Wedge

This chart pattern refers to either a reversal or continuation pattern. It slants either downward or upward and takes three to six months to develop.

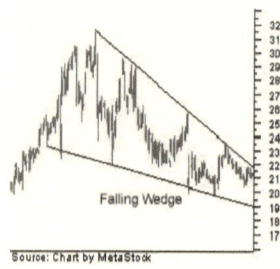

Source: Chart by MetaStock

It is a confusing pattern because it can be both a reversal and a continuation. A falling wedge is a bullish pattern while the rising wedge is a bearish one. If the asset price goes above the upper trend line, the chart forms a continuation pattern. On the other hand, it is a reversal pattern if the price moves below the lower trend line.

Triple Tops and Bottoms

The triple tops chart and the triple bottoms chart are not as popular as the other charts. They are similar to the double tops and bottoms, and head and shoulders patterns. For these two chart patterns, the asset price must touch the support or resistance levels thrice without breakthrough. The triple tops and triple bottoms signal a reversal trend.

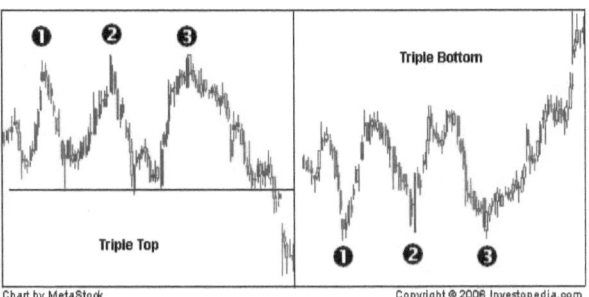

Rounding Bottom

This is a chart pattern, which refers to a long-term reversal from a downtrend to an upward trend. It takes months to years for it to develop.

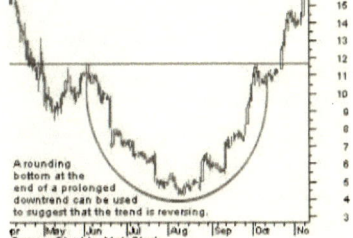

A rounding
bottom at the
end of a prolonged
downtrend can be used
to suggest that the trend is reversing.

Chapter 10

Getting What You Need to Start Day Trading

An obvious question that most people would want answers to relates to the basic things that a trader should have to begin day trading. Arguably, these are basic things that any trader should be aware of. This makes it important to take a look at some of the prerequisites that you will need to begin day trading.

Day Trading Broker

One of the biggest decisions that you will make in day trading is choosing an ideal broker. The broker that you choose will make a huge difference to the activity that you will be engaging yourself into. As a matter of fact, ideal forex trading strategies might not get you anywhere if you will be dealing with an unscrupulous trader. If they run off with your earning, what will you do? All your hard work would be washed down the drains. Therefore, it is vital for you to find a broker with a proven track record. The following tips should help you in finding a reputable broker to deal with.

Reflect on Your Needs

The first step that you should take is to reflect on the needs that you have with regards to your day trading ambitions. Consider whether you are going to day trade for long. Are you going to trade on small moves or big moves? If your goal is to day trade for long with the idea of capturing small moves, then it would be best for you to go for an ECN broker. This refers to a broker that makes use of electronic communications networks (ECNs) to offer their clients access to other individuals in currency markets. The benefit gained from an ECN broker is that they bring together price quotations from various market participants. Therefore, as a client, you will have tighter bids.

Well, if you will not be relying on an ECN broker, there are a wide array of others left for you to choose from. Depending on the type of trade that you will be engaging in, it is highly likely that you will settle for a varying broker. Do you remember the topic on capital requirements? Without a doubt, some brokers will have a higher minimum balance requirement whereas others will offer reasonable prices. For that reason, you should settle for a broker whose capital requirements meets your budgeted capital.

Which method of depositing or withdrawing money do you prefer to use? Brokers also have varying depositing and withdrawing options for you to choose from. If you are not comfortable with the common options provided by a particular broker, you simply need to move on to the next one. Your needs should be met by the broker that you will be working with.

Consider What the Broker Offers

Now, after reflecting on the needs that you have at hand, you should have selected a number of brokers that meet those needs. This means that your list should have reduced to a few brokers that you think they are potential candidates to help you in day trading. The next thing in line should be to consider what the broker offers. An essential consideration would be a broker that offers no dealing desk.

What is "no dealing desk?" This refers to a form of forex trading where the trader is granted with immediate access to the trading market. The benefit gained when working with a trader that offers no dealing desk is that there is no conflict of interest that could ensue with your local trader. At times there are instances where the broker would want you to lose.

Also, there have been numerous cases where brokers have been accused of using their customers' trades. Therefore, the idea of no dealing desk avoids all these issues.

The exciting thing about no dealing desks is that it also helps you avoid the common delays which could be brought about by the broker's delays in buying or selling securities for you. When a broker fails to buy or sell a particular security on time, this hinders you from making the best out of market opportunities that present themselves. These time delays are really frustrating more so for a new trader looking to make profits quick.

Another area that you would want to confirm with your broker is whether they are appropriately licensed and regulated. Notably, the issue of regulation is what you should pay attention to. Ideal brokers are those that are regulated by established financial systems. When dealing with forex, a broker who has Cyprus regulations covering them is better than working with one that lacks any.

Most importantly, the best broker in the market would be one that is always available whenever you need their assistance or certain clarifications. To know whether you are working with a broker with such attributes, open a demo account with them. Begin by sending them emails featuring the questions that you would like answered. While doing this, you should monitor their response rate. If their response rate is not something that astounds you, eliminate the broker from the list of your prospective candidates.

Check Their Reviews

An additional requirement when doing your research for the best brokers in the market is for you to consider their reviews. With the numerous social platforms discussing online trading, there is a certainty that you will find some information relating to the broker that you are thinking of working with. While going through these reviews, you should confirm that the reviews are from credible sources. This means that not all good reviews will be genuine. Be wary of fake reviews. Go through what many people are saying about the broker. If most genuine reviews feature positive reviews, then the broker is worth trying.

Test the Broker

After going through your needs and checking out what the broker offers, their reviews will give you some insight into whether they are reliable or not. Thereafter, you shouldn't make your decision yet. It is imperative for you to test the brokers. This is something that you should do on your own considering the fact that you will be dealing with them in the future. So, how do you test your broker for reliability?

Your first step should be to open a demo account where you will check out what their trading conditions are. The orders that you place from the demo account ought to be executed immediately. The platform being used should also be stable without any lags. If you are testing the product on your smartphone, the platform should not crash. Also, consider whether the spreads are tight enough.

After trying the demo for a week or two, you can go ahead to open a live account. This applies in cases where you had a smooth experience using the demo account. If not; you should try out another demo account from another broker that you were considering. With your new live account, you should deposit a fraction of the initial capital that you had budgeted for. Begin trading with the small percentage of your capital to see how things go for another week. During this period, your aim should be to test the customer care support that your broker offers. Within the same week, try to withdraw some money from your account. You should also find out whether the withdrawal process is easy and whether the broker charges for withdrawal are reasonable.

When the assessment is over and you think that the broker meets your demands, you can go ahead and continue using the live account that you had created.

Stay Away from Bonuses

Most traders would be swayed to go for bonuses that brokers offer. It should be pointed out that there is nothing which comes on a silver platter. Nothing is free in this world. So, expect that there is a hidden benefit that the broker would gain if you accepted the bonuses being offered. To refrain from using these bonuses, email your broker informing them that you are not interested with the bonus promotions being offered.

A Reliable Trading Account

As you continue with your search for an ideal broker, you should consolidate this process with finding a reliable account for your online trading. The following are pointers that should help you in finding a good account that will give you a smooth experience while day trading.

Don't Disregard Others

After getting recommendations from your friends on the best trading accounts, you should not automatically disregard checking what other accounts have to offer. One thing that you should always remember is that it is your personal needs that matter the most. Consequently, the best trading account for you should be one that suits your trading needs.

User-Friendly Interface

The other thing that you would want to confirm is whether the account offers you with a friendly interface. The features incorporated within the account should be easy to use. The first glimpse of the platform should give you the answer as to whether you want to use it or not. If you don't like how it looks, then look for another one.

Functionality and Additional Features

The many features included within a particular account

should not lure you into concluding that the account is worth using. You should realize that some of the features will not help you in any way. There are those that you might never use. So, try to look at the functionality aspects of the trading account. Consider whether the features being offered are important and necessary. The last thing you need is to complicate your trading experience. As such, go for an account that is simple to use and understand.

Stability

If you are using your smartphone to trade, the account provided should be stable. Applications which are constantly crashing will deter you from enjoying the trading experience. Therefore, before you rely on a specific account, make sure that you test it for stability.

Support from the Broker

Your broker should be ready to work with the account which you would have chosen. The customer care support that you get from them will make a huge difference to your trading experience. In this case, they should be highly responsive to any queries relating to the trading activity you will be indulging into.

A Charting Software

Your trading business would be made easier with the help of charting software. If you are new to the world of online trading, you must be wondering what a charting software means. Basically, this is a software which will help you with analyzing markets. It is a computer-based tool that aid forex traders to analyze currencies prior to buying or selling them. With the help of this software, a user would easily see graphical shifts in the currency values within a particular trading period. Usually, the information provided in these charts vary. Some info could be detailed whereas others could be simple. In both cases, the details provided are essential for technical analysis.

When looking for a day trading charting software, quality should always be an important consideration. It should be noted that this is a personal decision that should be made by purely looking at one's needs. A software that other traders think is ideal might not be the best option for you. The software that you choose should have the features that you think you will need to conveniently trade. What are some of the features you should look for in a charting software?

Real-Time Data
The best software to use is one that offers real-time data for you to make sound conclusions on whether to buy or sell. It is essential that you use a demo software which will not have any delays.

An Array of Indicators
Your needs should also be met by the array of

indicators that the software provides. If you prefer to use Japanese candlesticks, bar charts or point and figure charting, all these should be featured in the software of your choice. These indicators will come handy during technical analysis.

Competitive Rates

Beyond doubt, a new trader will want to settle for software that will not cost a lot of money. An ideal software should be reasonably priced. The best way of landing on a good charting software is to shop around. Don't just settle for the first software that you find during your search. However, it should also cross your mind that cheap is expensive. Therefore, you shouldn't be convinced that the best software is one that is free. Remember, you get what you pay for. As such, it is vital for you to consider your needs while making sure that a software provider offers just that.

Trustworthy Software Companies

The best provider will be one that has a proven track record. The software provider you will go for should have a positive image over the internet. Therefore, you might want to go over reviews for the software company before signing up.

To help you get started, we have compiled for you a list of some of the best charting software that you can rely on in the market. A succinct description is also provided to ensure that you know what to expect from the software providers.

TradingView

Below is a glimpse of how TradingView charting software looks like.

Source: "Live Stock, Index, Futures, Forex and Bitcoin Charts on TradingView."

TradingView is reliable charting software that you can try out. The good thing about this platform is that it offers you the opportunity of accessing a wide array of markets. Therefore, you will not only be limited to the stocks market, but you also garner the advantage of trading in futures, bond quotes, and forex. To new traders, they can also try out the charting software by using a free account.

Concerning its features, the software gifts you with an array of indicators to help you in making an accurate market analysis. The provider has incorporated a social community where one can source for trading ideas from those with experience.

MetaStock

Source: "MetaStock D/C.".

Another software that comes highly recommended is MetaStock. This is a software that works bes for traders who carry out their analysis after markets have closed. With the wide array of analysis tools that the software provides, the tool could be used by both experienced and new traders. Moreover, there are several markets including bonds, forex, futures, stocks, options and several others that a trader can exploit to meet their financial goals.

TeleChart (TC2000)

Source: TC2000 (TeleChart)

Another great software that is highly ranked over the internet is the TeleChart which is often referred to as the TC2000. Most reviews over the internet will point out that this software is pure gold when i comes to charting. The software is not free, but with the different plan options that it offers, you can stick to a payment plan that suits your budget. Among the best features, you can expect is the user- friendly interface, the array of drawing tools and the several customizable features. The only disadvantage of using this software is that you will not access it until you pay the subscription fee required. But then again, remember the fact that you pay for what you get. Considering the positive reviews it has over the internet, it is a platform worth trying.

Optuma

Source: Optuma. "Optuma for CMTA Members."
Optuma stands as one among the best platforms to use not just because of its excellent pricing strategy but because of its ideal technical analysis tools it offers. There are over 400 indicators and drawing tools that any user can exploit. This means that you can choose any chart types that you think will make it easier for you to analyze a particular market.

If the software provider offers you with a demo option, ensure that you utilize it to test the software before using it. This will help you in finding appropriate software that meets your trading demands.

Chapter 11

Day Trading Mistakes to Avoid

Whenever you are starting any venture, you are likely to lose something or make some mistakes before you get a proper grasp of what you are doing. This is especially true for day trading though with day trading, the risks are higher. Here, the risks have to do with money, and this in itself is a challenge. This is because a day trader needs to be quick witted as well as skillful, to be able to purchase stocks and sell them within the same day, and hope that by doing so it is possible to make a profit from the minutest fluctuations in the prices of the stock over 12 hours.

Years ago, day trading was impossible for the average investor, as the tools that were needed were not available to them. These tools included real-time stock results, access to instant traders, and the tools for analysis. High-speed internet and Dutch courage have changed this scenario for many who are now willing to try their hand at day trading. There are certain things that need to be avoided though, even for the most strong-hearted new trader.

In day trading, making mistakes should be avoided as much as possible because even the slightest mistake can have a massive impact on total income. In order to avoid mistakes, you need to be aware of the mistakes that you could inadvertently make. That is what will be addressed in this section.

Starting Big

As a new day trader, it is likely that you are bubbling with enthusiasm as you look forward to starting your trades. You have read up on all the theory, including the trips and tricks and believe that you are ready for the game. If you have managed a sizeable capital portfolio from an investment, you may be keen to start big and make big profits.

Even with all the theoretical preparation possible, as a new trader, you need to learn and observe the practical aspects of day trading. With experience, you can take calculated risks.

For this reason, new day traders are advised to start small rather than starting big. This is because when you are likely to make the most significant mistakes in your trading career as you start out.

You need to start trading with capital that is minimal so that you can assess your success. After a while, and with your wits intact, you should be able to see successful trading with more than three contracts. At this point, you can consider increasing the amount of money that you invest each time, and this should help you get better profits.

Learn the Basics

Day trading is not something that you can simply teach yourself and then start excelling at. You need to get some hands-on advice from people who are seasoned day traders. To do this, you should find an experienced trader and spend some time observing them, asking questions, and listening to advice. Learn how to play the game of trading, so that you can build up the confidence to give it a good go yourself. Realize that this will require patience on your part so that it can be gotten right. With proper determination, you will find that your efforts are enough to lead to big profits.

Planning To Fail

Failing to plan is planning to fail, and this is especially true for day traders. Trading is about making a profit, and not about experiencing feelings of exhilaration by taking chances with money. In light of the outcome that is expected, it is important that all traders have a plan of action.

A plan is particularly important because of the speed and emotion that affect day trading. Day trading is likely to be backed into corners where they need to make instant decisions, or during a volatile day of trading, they could get caught up in the events of the day and make decisions that will negatively affect their bottom line. Have a plan in place, especially when it is in writing, is an important step to controlling day trading.

A day trader who has taken the time to create a plan which is detailed will understand what his overall goal will be and will mold behavior and actions to meet that goal. Within the plan, there should be information on what shall be traded and the markets that the trades will take place in. There will also be details on the methods that will be used for entry and exit into the markets. This will help the day trader avoid buying into a security which would not usually have been considered.

An excellent plan will also have a risk assessment section, with details on the proper reactions to a host of scenarios. This could include how to react adequately to an excellent day of trading, or how to deal with consistent disappointments. Either way, it is supposed to ensure that the trader remains on track regarding what is required.

Missing Discipline

The best managers, especially those who work in high-risk professions will often create a contingency plan, in case their original plan does not pan out. This means that they are ready for the unexpected.

In day trading, this type of planning is also necessary, particularly because this activity is highly emotional. Having discipline could be the difference between profit and loss.

An aspect of discipline includes stop-loss orders. These orders are triggered based on certain conditions within the day-trading market. They help investors to save money, particularly if the trade is taking place automatically. It is imperative that all traders have a plan that will help them to manage their risks, as well as their possibilities for success or failure.

Manage your Expectations

Day trading is not a get rich quick scheme. Neither is it a magical wand that will help relieve all of your problems. It is challenging, and there is the constant pressure that you could lose it all.

Rather than expecting to rake in dollars, expect to put in a significant amount of work in to perfect the method in which you trade. The reason for this is that success in trading requires a considerable amount of planning, together with hard work.

This planning requires an adequate input of time. Ideally, the time should be well spent observing leaders in the industry so as to discern their techniques.

Being Time Bad

Day trading is already chaotic because of the speed with which transactions are done. However, there is no time that is as busy and chaotic as the first and last 20 minutes of each day. This is because it is the period where investors are the most anxious, looking to make the fastest moves before everyone else appears, or at the end of the day.

As a new trader, this is an excellent example of volatility in the market. It would serve you better to simply wait, rather than join the hubbub. This way, you prevent yourself from making any detrimental mistakes, and you keep away from the competition from institutional traders.

Keeping Too Busy

Being busy is important, and many people want to be observed as being busy, as this is a way that they can validate the amount of work that they have had to do. In trading, being too busy is not good for a trader. It indicates that it is possible to let things slip through their fingers.

A new trader may attempt to manage at least 10 trades in a day. The assumption is by trading more, you can make more. This may not actually be the case. Some professional traders insist on trading just two trades through the day. They may complete the trades early in the day, but then they can spend the rest of the day following up. By having fewer day trades to monitor, it becomes easier to see when there is a change in the market.

If you are a new trader and have achieved success from doing two trades a day, you may be tempted to make more money by increasing the number of trades and trading more. The problem with this is that it may set you back and turn your profitability on its head. This is because you will be stretching your attention. Instead, try increasing the amount that you are trading on your two commodities or for your two investors.

Watch out for Losing Streaks

There is nothing that can be as disheartening as repeatedly losing when you are day trading. If you are not careful, it may reach the point where you end up being clinically depressed, especially if you are always losing more progressively. That is why even though you may have the enthusiasm to day trade on your own, you need to seek out council from a professional who has been successful. Over time, you will pass the phase of losing streaks, and the moments that you were demoralized will be distant memories.

Thinking Anyone Can Do It

Should you ever be in a car accident, and were in need of life-saving surgery, would you allow a teenager in high school to operate on you? Your answer is most likely, "Absolutely Not!"

If you had a large sum of money which you wanted to see grow, would you pass it to the first person that you walk by on the street and say, "I'll wait to hear from you." Of course, it's highly unlikely.

So, when you are looking for a day trader, you need to make sure on certain things, one of which is that the person is qualified when it comes to day trading. They need to have some training as well as possible certification. If you have made the decision to go into day trading without any help, then you also need to ensure that you are capable of making informed decisions. Make sure that you have mastered all the theoretical knowledge available and that you have watched an expert practically as well. Remember that you cannot rush the process. It is entirely possible that this could take several months.

Keep an Eye on your Risk Capital

There is every possibility that when you are trading your capital, you will lose everything. This means that you need to be able to distinguish between your normal capital and your trading capital. Your normal capital includes the money that you need for your day to day living, so that you can pay bills, have food to eat, pay your rent or mortgage, and have something decent stashed away for your retirement. Your trading capital is money that you are willing to risk. This is money that should be solely dedicated to day trading, and nothing else. That way, you lose it all, your life will not start to fall apart all around you. It is also noteworthy that a day trader is required to keep a certain amount in their account as equity, and the minimum must be maintained if there is to be any day trading taking place.

Messing up your Margin

Your capital as a day trader is likely to fluctuate up and down throughout the day. Sometimes, it is on the lower side, and you need an extra boost. So you choose to borrow from a broker so that you can purchase securities. This is meant to be a facility that gives day traders some wiggle room if it is used correctly. However, some people have used this support in the wrong way or have abused it. This could occur when one borrows much more than they can pay back, and the result is an empty trading account and the mounting of debt. As much as possible, day traders should trade within their means.

Ignoring Important Resources

Perhaps the most important asset that you can get that will lead you to success when day trading online is an excellent high-speed internet connection. Next is an investment in state of the art software that is specialized and fully loaded with a range of analysis tools. Then you should make sure that your trading wallet is well stocked, as you need a significant amount of capital to get you started. As part of your resources, you should have direct access to an expert in the field so that you can get advice when you need it, and also get input on your equipment and its specifications. Finally, hire yourself a coach. This will be a great investment, allowing you to learn what is necessary to master day trading for the long haul.

Forgetting About Mental Health

Having the right state of mind could be the difference between winning and losing. In order to come out on top as a winner, one who is competent and can trade on instinct, you need to learn how you can manage your emotions. So, you cannot allow the intense thinking and mental energy that goes into day trading bring you down and drain your energy. You have to be ready for action, always ready to make a move. This is like having a jerk reflex. With this as a trick up your sleeve, you will be able to gain competence and win consistently. It will build up your intuition so that you always aim for and attain trading success.

The more that you trade, the better you will become. You need to give yourself the gift of concentration when you are trading. This is so that you can create sweet trading music in your mind. Getting into the zone is something that the most successful traders are able to. It is the trance of trading, and it leads to success.

Chapter 12

Day Trading Risk Management

What is risk management?

Risk management is when you identify, assess and prioritize the risks that you may face. It is followed by applying various resources so that you can control and minimize the risk factors, while businessmen monitoring them. It also includes doing certain things so that you not only reduce the risk but also maximize your opportunities through effective application of resources.

For an everyday trader, it is essential not to risk too much money on any given trade. Unfortunately, most people don't see the risks, but only the potential rewards.

Give it a thought. If a trader was to lose a little bit of money on every transaction, won't he decide to stay for longer? Huge losses are one of the major reasons why so many traders give up. But then why do traders give up? If all big losses start small, isn't it easier to prevent this small loss from becoming uncontrollable? The answer is "YES."

Below we shall see the way to assess risks and hence manage them better.

The importance and benefits of risk management

One of the major disadvantages of investing money in the stock exchange is the risk that comes along with it. No one is guaranteed success in the stock exchange and you will need to jump into it knowing the risks. Once you assess the risks, you can take precautionary steps to manage these risks. Risk management is extremely important while engaging in day trading and it can make or break your trade. If you are someone who generally takes risks then the stock market is a place where you can invest. Always keep in mind that in day trading the risk doubles and be prepared to manage this risk.

Here are some benefits that day traders will gain once they understand the risks:

- They will be prepared to face financial losses and will have strategies in place to overcome these losses.

- They will learn not to keep their stocks overnight as prices change radically overnight.

- They will realize it's a stressful and time-consuming job and have effective coping strategies in place.

- They will realize that they can't take extreme risks with borrowed money.

- They don't believe in quick profits and promises. They realize that it will take time and effort.

- They pay close attention to trends and know when something works for them and when it doesn't.

Basic Risk Management in day trading:

- You should be aware of both the potential risks and rewards before you enter a trade. Make sure that the potential rewards outweigh the potential risks.

- You must cut your losses before they become too much. You can either do this manually or through a broker.

- Take position sizes that are appropriate for you. This varies from one trader to the next.

- Don't give in to your pride. This could be a reason for losing money. Everyone who works with the stock market faces losses in the stock market. Don't blame yourself for the loss.

Chapter 13
Think Like a Geek

The use of strategies alone is not enough. In order to further increase your chances of making a profit, you also need to observe the best practices followed by successful stock investors.

Sufficient Research

It is not surprising why so many people lose their money when they invest in stocks. Although books on the subject always emphasize the importance of doing research, only a few are able to research properly. Unfortunately, many investors think that simply because they have researched the market for two straight hours, then it would be enough foundation to come up with a sound investment decision. This is wrong. Make sure that you conduct a sufficient research. If you are serious about being a successful investor, then research should be a natural part of your day-to-day life.

Start Small

It does not matter how much money you have in your account that you can use for investing. When you are a beginner, you should always start small. In fact, it is recommended that you first use a demo account, so that you can test the water without risking any money. This will also give you a chance to learn how to properly navigate your broker's platform.

Always start small. Your objective is to familiarize yourself with the actual practice of buying and selling stocks, as well as to develop a winning strategy. Do not worry, once you have a reliable strategy in place, you can always increase the amount of your investment, which will also increase your potential profit.

Diversification

Diversifying your investment is one of the best ways to minimize your losses. As they say, you should not put all your eggs in one basket. The reason is that no matter how much you study the stock market, it can only increase our chances of success. But, it can never guarantee the return of positive profit. In fact, there is a possibility that you may even lose your investment. Investing in stocks has its risks, just like any other profitable investment opportunity. By diversifying your investment, you can lower your risk and minimize your losses.

There are different ways to diversify. The most common way is simply to purchase stocks from different companies and not place all your money in a single company. Another way is to diversify by industry. Industries rise, and fall and such is outside of your control. An industry that is well and blooming today may no longer be considered a profitable investment by tomorrow. Therefore, scatter your investment over different industries.

Asset class diversification is another way to diversify. You do this by investing in the different asset class, such as in bonds, stocks, commodities, and others. When you apply this strategy, you should learn how to time it well. For example, in case of an economic recovery, stocks may be your best asset to invest in. However, in case of recession, investing in bonds could be a better option than investing in stocks. Strategy diversification is another effective way to cut down your risk. Depending on where you want to invest or how you want to invest (short term or long term), certain strategies may be more applicable than others. For example, in case of a long-term investment, you simply cannot neglect the use of financial analysis. In the case of a short-term investment, technical analysis may be one of the best strategies that you can use. You might also like to use geographic diversification. Many investors are quite biased and only invest in companies that are located in a particular territory. Take note that there is no industry in a specific geographical location can outperform others continuously. Ups and downs are normal in the stock market. You can also diversify as to time. Take note that you do not need to invest all the money in your account in one day. You can scatter your investments over time. For example, you can invest 20% of your money today and then follow it up with a 30% next month. Just like anything in business, proper timing is essential to success.

Diversifying simply means spreading your investment and not placing it in a single basket. Take note that diversifying alone is not a key to profit. One important part of diversifying is choosing where to diversify and place your money. Therefore, you cannot sacrifice the importance of doing research and analysis.

Avoid following Expert Advice all the time

When you are a beginner, you may find it helpful to search the net for pieces of advice coming from the so-called "experts." This is a common mistake because not all of these "experts" are real experts. These days, it is fairly easy to spread a word and promote one's self online. In fact, if you are good at marketing, you can easily project an image that you are an expert stock investor even if you have not invested in a single stock in your life. It is also worth noting that even the real experts also commit mistakes from time to time.

The best way to avoid relying on expert is to develop your own understanding of the stock market. After all, what separates an expert from a complete beginner is that an expert has his own view of the stock market and is able to support his view with reasonable defenses, while a beginner usually relies on what other people say. Of course, this does not mean that you should never take the time to read or listen to what the experts have to say. Rather, this only means that you should take every message or advice with a grain of salt. Instead of relying on what experts have to say, you can use their views as additional references to help support your own investment strategy.

Beware of the Pump and Dump Scheme

The pump and dump is a common scheme that you should watch out for. Unfortunately, although people are aware of it, many still fall for this fraudulent scheme. So, how does it work? A business or person who owns stocks promotes his stocks and spread positive rumors about them. This is a promotional hype that oversells the value of the stocks. This will tend to draw more attention to the stocks. In turn, this will increase the price of the stocks. When this happens, other investors will offer to buy the stocks thinking that they are a good investment. Now, after the sale of the stocks, the promotion and bad rumor will stop. The price of the stocks will then begin to dwindle down. After all, the true value of the stocks is lower than its value or price during the promotion. The end result is that the seller of the stocks makes a profit, while the buyer possesses a stock whose price is uncontrollably falling down.

Take note that the pump and dump scheme is not a completely bad thing. As you can see, you can take advantage of it and earn a profit. The key is to buy the stocks before or immediately right after the initial part of the pump and dump scheme. You then have to sell them just before their value begins to drop. The best way to do this is to sell the stocks after you see even just a small amount of profit. Do not wait for the promotion to stop. After all, such is outside your control.

Do not Hold On to the Stocks for Too Long

It is worth noting that not all investors lose their money for picking the wrong stocks. Some lose their money because they pick the right stocks but hold on to them for too long. Do not underestimate the volatility of the stock market. Make sure to sell your stocks before their price drops. Take your profit while you still can.

Understand Volatility

You should have a right understanding of what volatility is. Many people think of volatility as something where the prices of stocks simply rise and fall almost randomly. They often think that after a big rise, then a massive fall can be expected, and vice versa. However, this is not always the case. If it were so, then volatility would be something that is easy to predict. The volatility of the stock market is influenced by various forces. This means that even after a massive drop in the prices of stocks, it is still possible that another drop will take place. This also means that the result of a

particular trade is independent of past trades or transactions. Unfortunately, some people think that since their last three investments did not work out, then it is most probably that the next trade will end up with a favorable outcome as long as they use the same strategy. However, this is wrong. In fact, there is a good chance that the subsequent trade or investment will also be a loss. The reason lies in the strategy that you are using. If the strategy keeps on losing, then it is a sign that you should change or at least modify your strategy. True professional investors do not rely on mere luck. They know that if they come up with a true winning strategy, then the chances of raking in some profits would be high. Take note that even if you have a good strategy, there is still a chance that you may lose an investment. After all, there is no strategy that can guarantee 100% the return of positive profits. But, with consistent research, hard work, and practice, you can tilt a favorable outcome to your side and establish a winning edge over the stock market.

Keep a Trading Journal

Although not required, keeping a trading journal can be beneficial. Do not worry; you do not need to be a professional writer to maintain a trading journal. However, you do need two things: One, you need to be completely honest. This means that you should admit and accept your strengths and weaknesses, as well as the outcome of every investment that you make without any bias. And, two, you need to update your journal on a regular basis.

Your trading journal can contain any information that you want that is related to your life being an investor. Ideally, you should write in your journal the reasons why you want to invest in stocks, as well as your short-term and long-term goals. This is something that you can come back to in the future in case you get lost or confused along the way. Your journal should also include your strategies, the investments that you make, and your objectives. Simply put, your journal is as meaningful as you make it.

It is recommended that you write as much as you can in your journal. The reason is that your journal should serve as an unbiased mirror that will allow you to view yourself from a different perspective. It will make it easier for you to spot any weakness or part of your strategy that still needs to be modified. There are many things that your journal can teach you. Again, the important thing is for you to be completely honest with every detail that you write in your journal, and update it regularly.

Do NOT Approach Investing as a Hobby

The sad truth is that most people who invest in stocks approach the stock market as a hobby. Although you are always free to consider it a mere hobby, you can also expect to get a fair result just as when you approach any other business as a mere hobby, without any commitment or dedication. If you want to get a good amount of regular income from your investment, then you should take it as a business or a profession. The problem with those that consider this kind of venture as mere hobby is that they fail to exert the right amount of effort and research that will enable them to increase their chances of making a profit.

Wait it Out

Sometimes the best way to deal with the stock market is simply to wait it out. It is inevitable that you will soon encounter a time when the market is simply going down. Instead of being too bothered and placing risky investments, just wait it out. Waiting things out does not mean that you would completely ignore the market. It means that you should still follow what is happening in the market, but do not make any move or investment. Wait for the right time to act. When the market recovers, then be sure that you are there to take advantage of it.

Do NOT be an Emotional Trader

Although it is good to have passion in what you do, you should not allow your passion or emotion to get in the way and cloud your judgment. When you make an investment, it is not enough that you feel good and confident about it. Rather, you should feel confident of your trade because you have done the right research and study, and that there are good reasons to believe that it is the best investment. When you allow your emotions to cloud your judgment, you will not be able to think clearly. Therefore, at any time that you feel like your emotion is getting in the way of your decision making, stop and do not place any investment whatsoever. Wait for the undue emotion to disappear before you make a move.

Take Advantage of a Bull Market

A bull market describes the stock market. It signifies that the prices of stock in the market are rising — which is good. On the contrary, when the prices are falling, then it is called as a bear or bearish market.

You should learn to take advantage of a bull market. Of

course, the key here is to be able to recognize that a bull market is the current situation of the market or when a bull market is just about to take place. You need to place your positions (investments) as early as possible so that you can take advantage of the rise in the prices of stocks. A bull market usually takes place after a bearish market. It is important for you to recognize as quickly as possible when a bear market would end and a bull market to begin. To do this, you need to keep up with your day-to-day research and analysis. Although a bull market may be promoted on the news, the best way to take advantage of it is by placing your investments at its inception. The reason is that a bull market is usually followed by a bearish market. If you wait for a bull market to be announced before you act up, then it may already be too late for you. Take note that the way to be ahead of the stock market is to be ahead of the competition. Be the first to grab every opportunity.

Test and Develop your Strategy

Always test your strategy, and test it multiple times before you use it with real money involved. Take note that you have to repeat this process even if you just change or adjust a minor part of your strategy. A good way to do this is by using a demo account or by investing the minimum amount.

When you are a beginner, a big part of your time should be spent on developing a reliable strategy that can earn you some profits. It is advisable that you should focus on increasing your success rate. Take note that as a beginner, your main objective is not to earn money right away. Your first concern is to develop a winning strategy. Of course, a winning strategy depends on the situation, as well as on the amount of research that you make. When it comes to success in the stock market, the more information you have, the better is your chances of hitting the right investment. Do not rush. It takes times to know the best investment decision.

Never Chase After your Losses

This is a common advice given to gamblers: Do not chase after your losses. A quite surprising truth about this is that most people who chase after their losses are well aware of this advice. But, despite the knowledge that it is not a good practice to chase after one's losses, they still fall into this pitfall.

Investors usually get strongly tempted to chase after their losses after a big loss. After a big loss, you simply cannot think clearly. Hence, even if you know that chasing after your losses is not a good idea, you may get tempted to rush and do everything to get back what you have lost. In the process, you will probably lose all your money. Therefore, so that you will not lose control of yourself, make sure to have the strength to stop making any investment when you encounter a significant loss. In fact, give yourself a time to forget everything about the stock market. People usually chase after their losses by placing a bigger investment with a hope that they may be able to recover what they have lost and also win even a bit of profit. After all, they have already invested some times and effort. The key here is that instead of chasing after what you have already lost, you should stay calm and focus on your winnings or profits. Take note that every investment that you make is unique from all the rest. Therefore, when you encounter a loss, just admit and accept the loss, and move on. After all, even the best strategy in the world will also lose from time to time. The important thing is for you to end up with a positive profit once you add up everything.

Only Invest the Money that you can Afford to Lose

Another common advice given to gamblers is to only play with the money that you can afford to lose.

Well, although you will not be gambling, you must realize that this is still an investment. And, like any other investment, there is a chance that you may not earn anything or even lose all your money. Therefore, to be safe, you should not use the money that you need to pay for your obligations, such as the money for your household expenses. It is also not advisable to borrow money from other people. This is to protect you from being drowned in debt in case the worst thing happens. You can, however, partner up with someone, if you need more financial backing.

Do NOT Give Up

The best stock investors have their own bad stories to tell. They have many experiences of being defeated in the stock market. However, they are the ones who have survived the challenges and have won the competition. As you journey and spend more time investing in stocks, you will also face numerous challenges. The important thing is for you not to give up and to learn from your mistakes. The stock market is not your enemy. In fact, it is your goldmine for profit. Your only enemy is yourself. You should exercise discipline and professionalism. When you encounter some bad streaks, you need to stay strong and give yourself time to recover. Do not give up.

Relax

Give yourself a break. It is so easy to get addicted to the stock market, especially when you see some profits coming in. However, you need to give yourself time to relax. Remember that you can come up with better investment decisions if you allow your mind to rest. Also, it takes time to earn a significant profit in the stock market. Therefore, give yourself time to relax from time to time, and then come back to work stronger.

Conclusion

Just because you've finished this book doesn't mean there is nothing left to learn on the topic, and expanding your horizons is the only way to find the mastery you seek.

Now that you have made it to the end of this book, you hopefully have an understanding of how to get started day trading forex, as well as a strategy or two, or three, that you are anxious to try for the first time. Before you go ahead and start giving it your all, however, it is important that you have realistic expectations as to the level of success you should expect in the near future.

While it is perfectly true that some people experience serious success right out of the gate, it is an unfortunate fact of life that they are the exception rather than the rule. What this means is that you should expect to experience something of a learning curve, especially when you are first figuring out what works for you. This is perfectly normal, however, and if you persevere you will come out the other side better because of it. Instead of getting your hopes up to an unrealistic degree, you should think of your time spent with the forex market as a marathon rather than a sprint which means that slow and steady will win the race every single time.